simply gemstones

Designs for Creating Beaded Gemstone Jewelry

NANCY ALDEN
COFOUNDER OF BEADWORKS

simply gemstones

Designs for Creating Beaded Gemstone Jewelry

POTTER
CRAFT

NEW YORK

Published in the United States by Potter Craft,
an imprint of the Crown Publishing Group,
a division of Random House, Inc., New York.
www.crownpublishing.com
www.pottercraft.com

POTTER CRAFT and colophon is a registered
trademark of Random House, Inc.

Library of Congress Cataloging-in-Publication Data
Alden, Nancy.
Simply gemstones : designs for creating beaded gemstone jewelry /
Nancy Alden.—1st ed.
p.   cm.
Includes index.
ISBN 978-0-307-45135-4
1. Jewelry making. 2. Beadwork. I. Title.
TT212.A524 2009
739.27—dc22   2008043248

Printed in China

Series Design by Lauren Monchik
Design by La Tricia Watford

Photography by Jennifer Lévy

10 9 8 7 6 5 4 3 2 1

First Edition

CONTENTS

INTRODUCTION

Do not let the word "gemstones" scare you. Don't get flustered by the implications of the words "precious" and "semiprecious." Despite the well-nurtured illusion that such descriptions are mostly reserved for transactions between the rich and their jewelers, the truth is that every reader of this book can afford gemstones, and every reader can make her own gemstone jewelry.

This probably won't diminish the number of women staring longingly into the windows of Tiffany's or stop the truly wealthy from seeking the advice of their jewelers about those "special" gemstones. But it will, I hope, open the eyes of many women to the limitless possibilities of creating their own gemstone jewelry, no matter what the limitations of their purses.

Because the range of gemstones is so vast, they adapt themselves to an equally large array of budgets. Many hundreds of different minerals, most natural, some human-made, are sufficiently endowed with inherent sparkle, radiance, color, texture, pattern, luster, luminescence, and other lovely qualities to be candidates for the cutting and polishing that turns them into gems. From humble hematite chips to prima donna diamonds, the huge selection of types, qualities, sizes, and shapes offers something for every budget. Even better, virtually all types of gemstones are available with the convenience of a drilled hole—in other words, they can be bought as beads. Using gemstones in jewelry is no longer the sole province of goldsmiths and silversmiths. Gemstones can now be "set" by simple threading onto strings and wires. Even diamonds, the hardest of gems and, until recently, reluctant to enter the realm of beads, have now succumbed to the power of the laser drill.

Although other materials can provide as much color, texture, and even glitter, there is something irresistible about gemstones. Whether costly or inexpensive, they have always exerted an emotional influence, and the lust for jewels seems to be a common desire throughout all cultures and all periods. Managing that desire within the confines of a reasonable budget is something that is easier to do when you are your own jeweler.

Whether your gems are precious, semiprecious, or hardly precious at all, that they are real stone always brings some satisfaction, for gemstones have a certain inexpressible quality, an emotional warmth that springs, perhaps, from their earthy and tactile character. Because they are the very stuff and substance of our planet—nature in one of its most glamorous aspects—we feel an attraction to them that goes beyond simple aesthetics. Although I have never placed faith in the mystical or healing properties of gemstones, I can understand those who do, and I am sometimes tempted by the thought that my "birth-stone" might actually have some special connection with me, or that those crystal beads lying close at hand could be replenishing the energy I need to write this book.

But, as a jewelry designer, I really don't need my gemstone beads to exude any metaphysical qualities at all. They offer an infinite variety, a way to express all moods and fashions: classical, whimsical, dark, bright, serious, playful, somber, or joyful. Whether they are designed as simple statements of good taste or as ostentatious clusters of glitter, gemstone necklaces, earrings, and bracelets make the woman wearing them feel a little brighter and offer an extra dash of beauty for others to enjoy. This book helps you create your own gemstone jewelry, gives you the satisfaction of expressing your own fashion sense, and saves you money. It is my hope that it also introduces you to the wider world of gemstone jewelry and gives you an idea of the wonderful variety of gems that deserve your attention. It is true that diamonds may be many girls' best friends, but there are a host of other jewels that want to get to know you!

gemstone basics

ABOUT GEMSTONES

If you have only a hazy understanding of what makes a "stone" into a "gemstone," you have plenty of company. There are, quite literally, hundreds of types of gemstones, and new ones are being "discovered" and "created" every year as the potential of previously scorned minerals and new technologies is recognized and exploited. Although the market knows a gemstone when it sees it, dictionaries and reference books offer paltry guidance in their definitions. Descriptions include: "a rock that can be cut and polished to be used for jewelry," "an attractive and valuable piece of mineral," "a stone that exhibits qualities of brilliance, luster, fire, etc.," and "a mineral with a crystalline structure." One authoritative guide even goes so far as to say, "There is no generally accepted definition for the term gem or gemstone." That gemstones are "minerals" and "rocks" is mostly undisputed, although these terms can also be imprecise. A mineral is inorganic, something neither "animal" or "vegetable" in nature; yet, both jet and diamonds start off as organic matter, amber is the fossilized resin of trees, and pearls are made by mollusks. Rock and stone are usually aggregates of minerals, but in the case of gem "stone" they can also be one single mineral or even a single element. Rocks are forms of chemical compounds created, with a few exceptions, by a geological process. They are forged in the earth by heat, pressure, and chemical reactions. They have a defined and compact molecular structure, often crystalline, which makes them hard. Along with hardness, they have other physical characteristics that make them relatively easy to identify.

But when is a mere mineral or rock a "gem" stone? When it is rare, perhaps, and found only in a few locations, such as larimar? But quartz is one of the most common minerals on earth and it is a gemstone! When it is crystal clear, such as, well ... crystal? But black onyx is utterly opaque and it is a gemstone! When it is very expensive perhaps, such as emerald? A fine strand of green emeralds could buy a container load of green aventurine, but the latter is also a gemstone. When it is more valuable than any other jewelry components? Yet some ordinary gemstone beads are cheaper than some glass beads! And even good-quality faceted beads can be less expensive than the best glass-crystal faceted beads.

So what, exactly, does define a gemstone? About the only things that all gemstones have in common is that they are hard enough to be polished (although some are not) and attractive enough that people want to use them in jewelry. Whether it is a "gem" or merely a rock is in the eye of the beholder and the judgment of the marketplace.

PRECIOUS OR SEMIPRECIOUS

Because the definition of a gemstone is so subjective and broad, there has traditionally been an effort to separate the "men from the boys," or "precious" from "semiprecious." The definition used to be quite simple—diamonds, rubies, sapphires, and emeralds were "precious" and all the others were in some way inferior, or "semiprecious." But, in today's gemstone market, a fine piece of imperial topaz has far more value than a similar piece of ordinary sapphire. Paraiba tourmaline is far more rare and expensive than most diamonds. Alexandrite is more valuable than most rubies.

One might think that these disparities could be rectified by adding more gemstones to the "precious" category, but the issue is further complicated by the fact that quality is everything. Some gemstones, such as rose quartz, can be found both at the very lowest end of the "semi" leagues, as well as mixing with the players in the "precious" teams, depending entirely on the quality of the individual piece. Equally, there are some sapphires and rubies that just don't make it in the quality stakes and are relegated to being extremely "affordable," if not downright "cheap."

Because the terms "precious" and "semiprecious" add more confusion than clarity, I don't use them, but I do try to define some of the properties of gemstones that create quality and value. The difference in cost and desirability between a 4mm hematite "gemstone" and a 5 carat diamond "gemstone" is immense, and this chapter explains why.

THE NATURE OF GEMSTONES

The physical nature of gemstones is a subject that appeals more to rock collectors, scientists, and gem merchants than it does to jewelry makers, who are generally more interested in aesthetics than physics. Should you want to know that the chemical description of aquamarine is $Al_2Be_3Si_6O_{18}$, that topaz has perfect cleavage, or that the refractive index of iolite is about 1.54, there are many books available that list the exact chemical composition, crystal system, hardness, cleavage, refractivity, and other defining physical characteristics of gems. It is, however, interesting to have an understanding of the methods by which gemstones are identified, and it is sometimes useful to appear knowledgeable in the eyes of gemstone sellers, if only to have them understand that you are not someone who can be deceived by serpentine dressed up as jade or howlite pretending to be turquoise.

CRYSTAL STRUCTURE

Most, but not all, gems are crystalline forms of minerals. Just like crystals of common salt, their molecules are arranged geometrically in such a way that a series of flat surfaces is created. These crystals can be created in various ways—from the furnaces of molten magma or lava, under the immense pressure of the earth's crust, or even from watery solutions. Whatever their origins, all crystals have certain defined characteristics and fall within one of seven families or "systems," a feature that helps gemologists to identify them and cutters to avoid destroying them. All crystals, even diamonds, can break, and many tend to break along predictable lines. If a gem breaks cleanly along a certain plane, it is said to have good "cleavage." Many crystals have no cleavage at all, but all have distinct ways they "fracture," or break unevenly. Aside from making you sound clever if you can drop the terms "cleavage" or "fracture" into a conversation about gems, these terms are of no practical use to you and can be immediately forgotten. "Hardness" is a different matter.

HARDNESS

This quality of gemstones is so important that a simple scale was created to rank them from 1 to 10 in order of increasing hardness. On the Mohs scale, named after its Austrian inventor, the softest mineral, talc, can be scratched by a fingernail, whereas the hardest, diamond, can be scratched by nothing else except another diamond. For the proper care of jewelry and to understand what gems are appropriate companions when creating a design, it is important to know a little about their relative hardness. For example, once you are aware that fluorite (Mohs 4) can be scratched by a knife, you will be sure not to store it with the cutlery nor set it on a strand between faceted beads of quartz, which, at 7 on the scale, is hard enough to scratch glass, which is a middling 5. Hardness is one of the reasons that diamond is the sole occupant of the royal throne of gemstones. Although rubies and sapphires clock in at an impressive 9 on the scale, they are 140 times less hard than diamonds, which rank at number 10. In general, I tend to think of any gemstone that can be scratched by glass, that is to say, less than a 5 on the Mohs scale of hardness, as being soft and requiring special care. Because anything less than 7 can be scratched by quartz, a component of common dust, gems in the 5 to 7 range category are hard but should be stored carefully. Stones of 8 or greater can generally look after themselves, but nothing should be allowed to rub against diamonds, which will damage the surface of any other gem. Hardness is, of course, one of the ways in which genuine stones can be distinguished from glass imitations because a gem scratches, yet is not scratched by, a material lower on the scale.

DENSITY

Density, or the weight of an object relative to its volume, is another useful way for gemstone dealers to distinguish one stone from another, and the range of specific densities of all gems is carefully charted. Measuring density, however, is not convenient for most buyers because it requires a hydrostatic scale or a series of heavy liquids, most of which are toxic. But, once you become familiar with buying gemstones, the weight of a strand can often tell you something about its nature. A strand of cubic zirconia (CZ), one of the densest of gems, is quite easily distinguished from a strand of similar glass crystal because the CZ feels much heavier in the hand.

COLOR

It is the properties of gemstones that are visible to the eye that are of overriding interest to the jewelry designer and to the wearer. Of these, color is often the primary consideration and seems to be a straightforward, inherent quality of the stone. Yet color is also a slippery character when it comes to identifying and categorizing gems. A single type of gemstone can exhibit a variety of colors or a range of tones, many of which are achieved through heat treatments or other enhancement processes. Indeed, classifying stones by color can cause confusion to both professionals and amateurs: sapphire comes from the Greek for "blue," and so it always used to be, but today sapphires come in many different colors—except red, when they are called rubies. Hematite comes from the Greek for "blood red," but it is dark gray. Diamond dealers refer to other gems as mere "colored" stones, but diamonds have always been found in shades of blue, black, and yellow, as well as the more typical "colorless." Turquoise is always blue, except when it's green; garnets are always red, unless they are "grossular," "spessartite," or "andradite." Aquamarine was once prized for its "sea green" color, but nowadays many people prefer its "sky blue" variety. The color "topaz" is a yellow-hued golden brown, but the gemstone also comes in blue, pink, and green. Kunzite and alexandrite change color depending on the angle from which you observe them, a quality called pleochroism. The word "amethyst" immediately makes you think "purple," but nowadays there is a

fashion for turning it green. Indeed, the moment you insist a gem is always a certain color, it is begging someone to show you that it's not. But if color is confusing to those who classify gems, it is a simple matter to those who use them—it is either pleasing or it is not. As a jewelry maker, your eye tells you most of what you need to know!

REFLECTION AND REFRACTION

The other essential quality of a gem is how it reflects light. All gemstones, particularly the opaque ones, depend on luster, or the way light reflects from their surface, for part of their effect. Luster ranges all the way from "splendent," reflecting all the light like a mirror, to "dull," reflecting hardly any light. In between is a range of effects described as "adamantine" (like diamond), "vitreous" (like glass), "metallic," "waxy," "pearly," "greasy," "resinous," and "silky." The majority of gemstones used for jewelry have a vitreous luster. Most transparent and many translucent gems also produce reflections from their internal surfaces. In the case of faceted transparent stones, the lower facets act like a mirror to reflect the light back up through the face of the stone. This is particularly important for colorless stones that are often cut to reflect the maximum possible amount of light from the lower facets, an effect known as "brilliance." Most gemstones also refract, or bend, light as it passes through them. This is useful to those who need to precisely identify gemstones—light bends differently in different types of gemstones and each finds its own position in an index of refraction. Some colorless gemstones also disperse light, breaking it into the colors of the rainbow, a quality that accounts for the "fire" in diamonds. Others achieve magical color effects through interference, where the light is broken into many different colors by the internal structure of the stone. These pleasant accidents of light—sometimes sparkling, sometimes subtle—include "iridescence," "opalescence," and "play-of-color." Precious opals and labradorite use this trick spectacularly, whereas pearls and moonstone content themselves with a more modest shimmering of hues. Occasionally, the internal structure of the stone reflects the light in a particular pattern, like the star effect of some rubies and sapphires, or the "chatoyancy" of all tiger's-eye.

INCLUSIONS AND OTHER "FLAWS"

Like all natural materials, gemstones exhibit natural variations, and it is seldom that any of them are completely "clean" of foreign matter, cracks, or irregularities in their structure. Although these used to be seen as "flaws," modern gem dealers understand that they can often be an asset. There is little doubt that a fifty-million-year-old insect encased in a piece of amber is an addition that makes the stone far more valuable than it would be without it. Some types of gemstone, such as rutilated quartz, even depend on their inclusions to provide value, whereas others such as lazurite look much better with specks of another mineral thrown in. Because the beauty of any gem is a matter of opinion, you should seek your own advice when deciding whether an inclusion is a mark of character or an unfortunate scar. Even cracks and cavities can sometimes lend an attractive character to a gem, but they are more often real flaws, marring the reflective qualities of the surface and weakening the integrity of the stone. Comparison with other qualities of the same gemstone helps you determine whether they add interest or cheapen the stone.

ENHANCEMENTS

In today's market, the entirely natural gemstone, untouched by any cosmetic treatment, is probably in the minority. The methods of enhancement have become so good and so difficult to detect that it is better for the buyer to assume a stone has been enhanced until proven natural. You can be certain that anything that can be done to make a gemstone more attractive will be done, whether it is oiling, waxing, heat-treating, irradiating, dyeing, acid-treating, coating, impregnating, reconstituting, or some technique that has only recently been invented and is still a mystery to the market.

Enhancement is not, in itself, a bad thing. The industry has come to accept that these treatments often improve gemstones and certainly deliver to the desiring public a far greater selection and quantity than would be possible without them. Indeed, some gemstones would not exist without enhancement: topaz is rarely found in a natural blue color; yet, wonderful shades, such as London blue, sky blue, and Swiss blue, have in the past few years begun adorning the necks of women around the world. The secret is the sophisticated heat treatment and irradiation of colorless topaz stones. Enhancement is positive unless it steps over the line of fair practice. That line is quite nicely drawn in the U.S. Federal Trade Commission guidelines that require a gemstone seller to disclose enhancements if it "has been treated in any manner that is not permanent or that creates special care requirements." Because most enhancements achieve permanent change, it is only those that fail or that are knowingly temporary that should concern the buyer. Unfortunately, there are plenty of those, and many cannot be detected until too late. Several years ago, a large quantity of chalcedony in India was subjected to a botched acid treatment, producing beautiful colors that were snapped up by dealers and customers around the world. It was only some months later that the colors began to fade and acid that had not been permanently combined with the stone began corroding the beading wires and findings. Ever since, I have bought and sold nothing but natural chalcedony, even though the coloring techniques are probably perfected by now. Few failed enhancements are quite as dramatic as that, however. Instead, over time surfaces become duller, colors paler. Of course, this also happens with some natural gemstones if they are not properly cared for. In the case of cheaper stones the fading of their charms might not be too bothersome, but it is certainly a major concern with more expensive gems and should be taken into consideration when purchasing.

THE DETERMINING CHARACTERISTICS OF A GEMSTONE

Chemical composition

Crystal structure

Hardness

Density

Cleavage

Transparency

Refractivity

Dispersion

Absorption

Primary color (streak)

SYNTHETICS

Synthetics are gemstones that are made in the laboratory or workshop. Often identical in composition to the natural stone, they are accepted additions to the supply of gems. Although there is hardly any stone that cannot be created synthetically, the high cost of production makes it economical for only the higher value gems to be created in the expensive furnaces of the laboratory. Another, less expensive type of synthesis is called reconstruction, and it is practical for some cheaper gemstones. In this process, the material is splintered or powdered and then heated and pressed to form larger pieces. Almost all hematite beads are made this way and turquoise, amber, lapis lazuli, and coral are sometimes given this treatment.

IMITATIONS

Because most gemstones have a vitreous, or glassy, luster and transparency, they are often imitated by glass, and it is sometimes difficult to tell the difference. Real gemstone frequently shows natural irregularity and inclusions that glass cannot match without time-consuming techniques, and there is often a perceived "life" in natural stone that glass can never quite imitate. Gemstones are also imitated by other gemstones, both natural and synthetic. Diamond is constantly being chased by other colorless stones that come close to mimicking its optical qualities, although its hardness has never been equaled. There is nothing wrong with any of these imitations as long as they are clearly described as such and not foisted off as the "real thing."

FAKES

Materials that masquerade as gems have been a problem in the marketplace as long as jewels have existed. Today, there is a good arsenal of techniques to distinguish fakes, but many of them require an inconvenient and expensive trip to the gemological laboratory. Small and inexpensive heat-resistance testers are beginning to become available, and these can be a good investment if you are producing a lot of gemstone jewelry. For the most part, however, you need to rely on the reputation of the seller to help you avoid an unfortunate purchase.

GEMSTONE BEAD CUTS

SMOOTH ROUNDS AND RONDELS

Almost all opaque gemstones and most of the colored transparent ones are available as smooth round or rondel beads. Some gems, such as iolite, peridot, garnet, and kyanite, are rarely seen in sizes greater than 4mm or 6mm. Most colorless stones are faceted to display their reflective properties better, although rock crystal and moonstone are also made into smooth rounds.

OTHER SMOOTH SHAPES

Many stones are cut as cabochons, circular or oval shapes with a domed front and a flat back, and set in gold or silver to form pendants. There are many other shapes of smooth gemstones that are drilled as beads. These range all the way from large ovals and lozenges, to small stars, crosses, and discs. The variety of shapes increases every year as inventive cutters explore the possibilities of different gemstones.

NUGGETS AND SHARDS

Sometimes, rough pieces of gemstone are tumbled to form polished nuggets or pebbles. If the crystalline structure of the stone is suitable, they can even be left unpolished in shards and whole crystals. These "rough" shapes can create interesting jewelry with a natural look.

FACETED ROUNDS AND RONDELS

These shapes combine the versatility of round beads with the increased reflectivity created by faceting. Transparent gemstones are not the only ones that are faceted; opaque stones like black onyx and even, on occasion, the natural smooth round shapes of pearls can be faceted as well.

(continued on page 16)

GEMSTONE BEAD SHAPES KEY

1. Onion-shaped briolettes (citrine)
2. Faceted discs (garnet)
3. Top-drilled marquise beads (peridot)
4. Faceted twisted box beads (labradorite)
5. Smooth round beads (golden rutilated quartz)
6. Flat faceted irregular beads (Sleeping Beauty Turquoise™)
7. Almond-shaped briolettes (rutilated quartz)
8. Faceted rondels (fire opal)
9. Faceted nuggets (Chinese turquoise)

CUTTING AND POLISHING

Pearls and a few gemstone crystals are attractive enough to be used in jewelry in their natural state, but the great majority of stones depend on the skills of cutters and polishers to make them into glittering gems. This process, which was traditionally and laboriously done by hand, is today accomplished with the assistance of partly automated or even fully automated machinery, but it still requires an expert understanding of the qualities of the gemstone. Gems can be destroyed or their looks cheapened by unskilled cutting, and decisions about how to achieve the greatest possible value from any piece of rough stone call for sophisticated judgment from cutters with many years of experience.

Many of the opaque and semitransparent stones are cut into rough shape and then turned on a lathe or in a ball mill to make them into round beads or domed cabochons. Then they are tumbled or polished so that their surface luster is revealed.

The true skill of cutting, however, is mainly practiced on the transparent stones that best display their optical qualities when they are faceted. Here, the gem maker must first decide which shapes to create on the basis of a balanced view of market demand and the most efficient way to use a particular piece of rough stone. Then he must determine the shape and number of facets that produce the most sparkle. Once he has arrived at a plan of action, each bead or stone must be cut individually. Despite the name "cutting," facets are actually created by wearing away the stone on a grinding wheel. With the exception of diamonds, which can only be ground by other diamonds, gems are faceted on a grinding wheel coated with carborundum, a synthetic form of the extremely hard gem moissanite. In the great gem cutting centers of India, some stones are still "hand-cut" using only traditional tools to help the eye guide the angles of the facets, but more and more gemstones are being "machine-cut" to achieve greater regularity and precision of both the facets and the overall size of the finished bead.

DROPS

Drop shapes are most often drilled sideways through the top or narrowest portion of the bead, but they can sometimes be found center-drilled where the hole traverses the entire length from top to bottom. The most common types of drops are teardrop or pear-shaped, almond, heart, onion, and marquise or double-ended. The last three shapes are flattened, presenting their widest aspect in two dimensions rather than three, and making the most economical use of the gem. Drops are as frequently faceted as rounds and in this more glittering state are often referred to as "briolettes." Another similar faceted shape is the "marquise," a type of drop pointed at both ends.

SPECIAL CUTS

The possibilities of faceting and shaping gemstones are still being explored and every year sees a creative new cut enter the marketplace. Some of these join the classic designs, whereas others enjoy a brief popularity in the ever-changing world of fashion.

CHIPS

Like sausages, chips are created from the leftovers after the main cuts have been removed. Cutting shapes from rough stone often involves wastage that, once sorted for size, tumble-polished, and drilled, is strung onto temporary strands and sold. And, like sausages, gemstone chips come in many different guises—some can be used for cheap and cheerful recipes, whereas others are sophisticated and serious elements of fine design.

VALUE

The value of gemstones is determined by several factors, primarily their popularity, rarity, and quality. With the exception of diamonds, which are subject to the controlling corporate influence of the De Beers group, prices are set by market demand. Because the market is so international, however, it is sometimes difficult to understand the causes of that demand; regional preferences play an important role in determining price, and gems tend to flow to the countries that value them most. A prime example of this is jade, which is fervently desired in China, but only modestly appreciated in the West. Few North Americans or Europeans can understand the fine gradations in quality or are willing to match the thousands of dollars that the Chinese are ready to spend on the best pieces. The sheer popularity of the stone among Chinese women pushes the prices of the best jade ever higher, while the women of the West, not so appreciative of the subtleties of this modest and discreet gem, are generally content to acquire the lesser qualities or give it a pass completely.

But popularity alone does not give value to gems—they must also be relatively rare, adding the problem of supply to the price equation. The variation in supply is enormous: some gems, such as Paraiba tourmaline, are found in the tiniest quantities in one or two places on earth, whereas others, to use the example of hematite (a form of iron oxide), are as common as rust. The consequence is that a single piece of the Paraiba tourmaline can cost as much as a house, whereas a nice strand of the hematite will set you back the price of a sandwich.

The most complex factor of value in gemstones, however, is quality. Even a relatively cheap type of gemstone can cost much more than an expensive one if its quality is superior. Because their livelihood depends on good judgment, dealers in gemstones have created sophisticated methods of measuring quality, methods that are often confusing and unhelpful to the layman who simply wants to purchase something that looks good. In the section Buying Gemstone Beads (page 137), I describe some of the ways professionals look at gemstone beads to determine their quality and value, as well as a simple method anyone can use to quickly gain some insight into the important relationship of quality to price.

THE PRODUCTION OF GEMSTONES

Gemstones are mined on every continent except Antarctica, but some areas of the world are particularly rich in these resources. Brazil, Burma, India, Afghanistan, Russia, Sri Lanka, eastern and southern Africa, and North America all have large-scale production of rough gemstones. In the case of diamonds, vast corporate investments have created huge open pit mines hundreds of feet deep, fringed by industrial complexes that sift through millions of tons of rock. But most other gems are mined more modestly, often by hand, in makeshift pits or shafts. Some, such as the opal mines of Australia are the territory of rugged individual treasure seekers, others are the enterprise of modern mining companies, and still others remain the traditional livelihood of remote communities. However the raw stone is wrenched from the ground, few gems are processed in the place they are mined. The rough gemstone is loaded into containers or barrels and shipped to the cutters and polishers of Europe and Asia. In recent years the former has been eclipsed by the latter, and even diamonds, once faceted in the workshops of Amsterdam and Antwerp, are now mostly cut in India. Traditional centers of gem cutting, such as Jaipur and Bangkok, still have thriving industries, but China, the leader in pearl production, has become the main producer of smooth round stones and is rapidly increasing its production of faceted stones. This vast international network of miners, cutters, and dealers offers today's jewelry designer an immense choice of gemstones in myriad shapes and sizes at many levels of quality and price.

GEMSTONE NAMES

Creating a list of gemstones is often a confusing business as many of them are known by two or more names. Compounding the difficulty is the fact that many seemingly unique gems are simply different aspects of one material.

For example, sapphires and rubies are both a gemstone called "corundum," a crystalline form of aluminum oxide. The only difference between them is that rubies are red corundum, whereas sapphires can be of many other colors. Jade, thought to be just one type of gemstone for thousands of years, was shown in the nineteenth century to be two separate minerals, jadeite and nephrite. Members of the garnet group don't even share the same chemical composition, although they all adhere to the same cubic crystalline structure and have similar hardness. Onyx, agate, and chalcedony are all quartz, as are the stones that are actually called quartz. Even the agreed names for stones have variations in spelling—some refer to one familiar form of garnet as "almandine," others say "almandite."

And added to all the variations of scientific and traditional names are the myriad titles bestowed on stones by sellers trying to make them sound more attractive. Thus, serpentine is commonly called "new jade" or "soo chow jade"; metallic pyrite, diminished by its nickname of "fool's gold," is often called "marcasite" even though that is the name of a completely different mineral; "Umba" sapphire really is a type of sapphire discovered in Africa's Umba River valley; "tundra" sapphire is neither found in the tundra, nor is it sapphire, but a particular color mixture of several other types of gemstone; and "water sapphire" is just a more romantic name for indicolite, a blue tourmaline. Even correct names can confuse. Peruvian opal is, indeed, a "hydrous silica gel" like its more precious cousin, but it has no play-of-color and no fire—in fact, it doesn't look the slightest bit like anyone's idea of opal. Then there are the blatantly false names, meant to confuse. Bohemian ruby for garnet, smoky topaz for smoky quartz, cherry quartz for glass, African emerald for green fluorite. It is enough to make one wish for some single authority to impose order. But sometimes the trade name is simply much better than the mineral name; we can all be thankful that someone had the bright idea of giving oligoclase feldspar the name *sunstone*, which delightfully describes its appearance. In the end, the market somehow arrives at the goal of assigning attractive names to beautiful gemstones, occasionally sidestepping a little confusion and deception along the way.

GEMSTONE BEAD SHAPES KEY
Opposite

1. Slice pendant (Chinese turquoise)
2. Faceted box (Swiss blue topaz)
3. Briolette (rose quartz)
4. Laser cut drop (garnet)
5. Laser cut flat drop (London blue topaz)
6. Large disc pendant (banded agate)
7. Carved leaf (serpentine)
8. Faceted chiclet (amethyst)
9. Cabochon set in silver pendant (aquamarine)
10. Faceted almond (labradorite)
11. Carved fish (carnelian)
12. Large faceted pendant (blue goldstone)
13. Carved flattened barrel (amethyst)
14. Center-drilled flat-bottomed drop (lemon citrine)

GEMSTONES USED IN JEWELRY

There are several hundred gemstones, many of which, due to their fragility or extreme rareness, are only of interest to collectors. The following chart describes most of the gemstones that are used in jewelry and are currently available in the marketplace as beads or pendants.

GEMSTONE	HARDNESS	COLOR(S)	REMARKS
agate	7	banded—many colors	commonly dyed
almandine (garnet)	7	red with a violet tinge	sometimes with a slight metallic luster
amazonite	6	blue-green	silky luster
amber	2	yellow-brown	resinous luster; often imitated by natural and synthetic resins
amethyst	7	purple	also heat-treated to create green amethyst
ammonite	4	brown with iridescence	the fossilized shells of extinct sea creatures
andalusite	7	brown-red, yellow-green	changes color in different light
apatite	5	green, blue, yellow	
aquamarine	8	blue, blue-green	heat-treated to achieve the best colors
aventurine	7	green to gold-brown	can be confused with "goldstone," a glass simulant
black onyx	7	black	a black type of chalcedony
bloodstone	7	dark green with red spots	
carnelian	7	orange, red-brown	vitreous to waxy luster; mostly dyed and/or heat-treated
chalcedony	7	blue, gray, white	other colors created through dyeing
charoite	5	violet with white veins	
chrysocolla	2	mottled green-blue and brown	vitreous to greasy luster
chrysoprase	7	apple green	vitreous to waxy luster
citrine	7	yellow, yellow-gold	most citrine is heat-treated amethyst
coral	3	red, black, white, and dyed colors	vitreous to dull luster; some varieties raise environmental concerns
cubic zirconia	8	many colors	a synthetic sometimes used to imitate diamond; very dense and heavy
diamond	10	colorless, black, brown, yellow, green	adamantine luster and brilliant fire
diopside	5	green	can be confused with emerald
druse	7	clear and other colors	crystalline interior of a hollow agate
emerald	8	green	usually oiled to improve surface; often clouded with inclusions
fire agate	7	orange-white with iridescence	
fluorite	4	mostly purple, but many other colors, often banded	
garnet	7	red	
grossular (garnet)	7	green	
hematite	6	gray-black	metallic luster; almost all hematite is reconstituted
hessonite (garnet)	7	syrupy brown	vitreous to resinous luster
howlite	3	white with black veins	porous and easily dyed; used to imitate turquoise
hypersthene	5	dark green	
indicolite	7	deep blue	a type of blue tourmaline
iolite	7	blue	
jade (jadeite & nephrite)	7	green, white, lilac	greasy to pearly luster; imitated by serpentine
jasper	7	many colors, striped, spotted or patterned	
jet	2	black	waxy luster; a form of coal
kunzite	7	lilac	

Note: Hardness indicates the approximate position on the Mohs scale of hardness. Stones with a higher hardness number scratch any of the ones below them in the scale. Glass has a hardness of 5 and any stones below that are considered to be "soft"; those of 8 or greater are very hard stones.

GEMSTONE	HARDNESS	COLOR(S)	REMARKS
kyanite	4 & 6	blue with streaks	vitreous to pearly luster
labradorite	6	gray-black with iridescence	best has a strong blue-green schiller
lapis lazuli	5	blue with brassy specks	vitreous to greasy luster; best is from Afghanistan; Chilean lapis is often dyed; the stone is imitated by sodalite and even glass
larimar (pectolite)	5	blue with white veins	best quality has more blue, less white
malachite	4	banded dark and light green	vitreous to silky
moonstone	6	white with blue or white opalescence	sometimes imitated by glass
morganite	7	pink	also called pink beryl or aquamarine
obsidian	5	black	a naturally occurring volcanic form of glass
opal (common)	6	blue, pink	same stone as opal, but without the play-of-color
opal (precious)	6	white or black with iridescence	vulnerable to drying and cracking
pearl	3	white, cream, golden, black and others	almost all are cultured; many are bleached or dyed
peridot	6	green	vitreous to greasy luster
prehnite	6	yellow-green	
pyrite	6	bronze-gold	metallic luster; called marcasite when set in silver
pyrope (garnet)	7	deep red	
rhodochrosite	4	pink with white veins	vitreous to pearly luster
rhodonite	6	pink with black veins	
rock crystal	7	clear	often sold in natural crystal shapes
rose quartz	7	cloudy pink	often dyed to improve the color
ruby	9	red	often dyed to improve the color
ruby zoisite	6	green with red inclusions	
rutilated quartz	7	clear with gold, black or red inclusions	the hairlike rutile is an opaque gemstone
sapphire	9	many colors except red	heat treatment produces a variety of colors
serpentine	5	green	vitreous to greasy luster; many trade names implying it is jade, which it is not
smoky quartz	7	brown-gray	
sodalite	5	blue with white veins	vitreous to greasy luster
spessartine (garnet)	7	orange-red	
spinel	8	black, red, blue	red spinel is sometimes sold as ruby
sugilite	6	violet	
sunstone	6	red-brown	
tanzanite	6	blue with purple and violet overtones	blue form of zoisite
tiger's-eye	7	brown-gold with chatoyancy	red tiger's-eye is dyed
topaz	8	yellow-brown, pink, blue, green	most pink and blue topaz has been heat-treated
tourmaline	7	many colors	
tsavorite	7	green	transparent form of green grossular garnet
turquoise	5	blue, green	waxy to dull luster; sometimes impregnated with resin (stabilized), sometimes oiled, sometimes reconstituted; imitated by dyed howlite; good synthetics are available; the stone is often faked
vesuvianite (idocrase)	6	green-brown	greasy luster
zircon	7	colorless, blue, yellow, red, brown, green	vitreous to adamantine luster

JEWELRY MAKING SUPPLIES

Before you rush out to buy any of the items listed below, carefully read the list of necessary ingredients and tools for the project you have in mind. Some require few tools or materials. In recent years, the proliferation of bead stores around the world has made it easy to acquire jewelry making supplies. If you do not have a local bead store, there are numerous mail-order suppliers, most of which offer online shopping.

TOOLS

It's surprising how few tools you need to make jewelry. For many necklaces and earrings, you can get away with just two: a pair of flat-nosed pliers and wire cutters. The other tools you need to make the designs in this book are detailed in "Toolbox Essentials" on the following page.

Some of these items you can find around the house, but you'll want to make a modest investment in tools specifically designed for jewelry makers because they will make your life easier and your finished jewelry better.

There are other specialty items you can add as you go along, but the items in "Toolbox Essentials" are all you really need. Some people like to lay out their necklaces on a bead design board that has specially designed curved channels for holding beads. If you don't want to purchase one, you'll need to work with a bead mat or some other thick, soft material to keep your beads from rolling all over the place.

Like everything in life, beading tools come in levels of quality. Their cost depends on precision, sturdiness, and durability. If you are on a budget or think that your enthusiasm for making jewelry might be short-lived, you can buy cheap pliers to get yourself started. When you are hooked by the satisfaction and pleasure of creating your own

jewelry, it will be time to upgrade—look for tools made in Germany. Once a passion for the craft sets in, you might want to splurge on a really superb set of Swedish cutters and pliers. But the important thing is just to get started.

SPACERS

Spacers are just beads that create spaces between other larger or more important beads. Theoretically, all beads can act as spacers. In practice, however, spacers tend to be fairly simple silver and gold beads, although they are sometimes more elaborate. Their most important characteristic is that they should emphasize, rather than overwhelm, the main beads. Spacers do not always do this by being restricted in number: sometimes they are used sparsely, and sometimes they comprise the majority of the design. Nor are they necessarily restricted in beauty. A whole strand of gold daisy spacers, for instance, can be a thing of pleasure. The spacers' position in the design determines their character. Spacers are beads that know when to hold back and let others take the central role.

STRINGING MATERIAL

The main structure of a neck "lace" is, by definition, a piece of thin material that can be wrapped like a lace around the neck. This material can be silk thread, leather thong, wire, chain, or one of the modern bead-stringing wires. Whatever the material, it must combine both strength and flexibility. Here are the stringing materials we recommend.

SILK

This traditional material is still preferred for threading beads and designs where the thread is to be knotted between the beads. It is reasonably strong, easy to work with, and very, very supple. While modern beading wire is stronger and easier to use, no other material allows a strand of beads to embrace the neck in quite the same way as silk. But silk has some distinct disadvantages: it will break when roughly handled, it will stretch over time, and it gets dirty. Because of this, any beads strung on silk will have to be restrung periodically. How frequently depends on how much you are wearing them. But a good rule of thumb is that necklaces that are worn regularly should be restrung every one or two years.

Silk comes in several thicknesses, which are expressed by an arcane alphabetical code. The thickest silk thread is FFF, while the thinnest is size 00. For our projects that require silk thread, we are going to use size F and keep things simple.

BEADING WIRE

Modern technology has tried to overcome the disadvantages of silk, while retaining its qualities of flexibility and ease of use. This was a surprisingly difficult task and the only material to come close is a relatively new and sophisticated product. Beading wire seems simple: it's just a few twisted strands of wire coated in plastic. But early attempts were frustratingly inadequate. The wire was too stiff to lie around the neck gracefully; it would kink if bent sharply and it would break if mishandled. The problems were solved by twisting more and more strands of thinner wire to add both flexibility and strength. Today's 19- and 49-strand beading wires are increasingly kink-resistant; they don't break under normal use and, although still not quite as supple as silk, they are very flexible. With the logic of an industry more used to hardware than jewelry, the manufacturers of beading wire have decided to measure its thickness in inches. This completely ignores the fact that the holes in beads are measured in millimeters. Wherever "beading wire" is called for in the materials list we recommend using the best quality 49-strand size .015. If a thinner or thicker wire is called for, it is specified in the list.

CHAIN

Whatever style of chain you prefer, I recommend that you use only sterling silver and gold-filled. Plated chain is cheaper, but deteriorates quickly and is not an appropriate material to use with gemstones. Solid gold chain is, of course, nice to have, but very expensive. In appearance and durability, gold-filled chain is the next best thing.

WIRE

Stringing beads together with wire is easier than it first appears. In these designs we use just two types: sterling silver and gold-filled, both in a "half-hard" density. Wire is sold in another traditional measurement, "gauge." The wires used in these designs are either 20 or 22 gauge, corresponding to .032 and .025 of an inch.

TOOLBOX ESSENTIALS

- Wire cutters
- Narrow flat-nosed pliers (also known as chain-nosed pliers)
- Round-nosed pliers
- Awl (for designs on silk thread)
- Crimping pliers (can be used instead of flat-nosed pliers to close crimps on beading wire)
- Scissors
- Beading needle (twisted wire)
- Hypo-cement glue (or clear nail polish)

FINDINGS

These linking pieces are the jewelry maker's essential hardware. Just as the carpenter fills his toolbox with the nails, screws, and bolts needed to construct his works, so the jeweler has her stock of clasps, wires, and links. There are hundreds of different findings, but you need know only a few to make the jewelry in *Simply Gemstones.* Most findings come in different metals, and you should always use the one that is appropriate to the design. The basic materials are listed below.

FINDINGS FOR NECKLACES

BEAD TIPS

Bead tips attach the end of a necklace thread to the clasp. The tip is designed to grip onto the knot you make after stringing the last bead, and it comes in two varieties, the basket bead tip and the clamshell. The former works by trapping the knot in a little basket, while the latter sand-wiches the knot between two concave wings that look like clamshells.

CLASPS

Clasps for necklaces and bracelets come in a staggering variety. Several different methods are used to attach the two halves of a clasp, but all the styles are attached to the necklace pretty much the same way.

CRIMPS

Crimps are tiny metal beads that can be crushed flat with pliers. Beading wire is first threaded through the bead crimp, then through the loop of a clasp, and then back through the crimp. Finally, the little crimp is firmly but carefully squashed to attach the wire to the clasp. There is even a specialty tool, crimping pliers, that helps exert the right amount of pressure to make a perfect seal. You can also close crimps with simple flat-nosed pliers.

CRIMP COVERS

These provide an easy way of disguising the messy part of the necklace between the clasp and the first and last beads. They are hollow spheres that open up like clamshells. You simply fit them over the flattened crimp and squeeze them gently shut. Once in place, they look just like a smooth round silver or gold bead. Although these findings are not necessary for the construction of a necklace, they can add an extra touch of sophistication to your designs.

FINDINGS MATERIALS

GOLD use only with gems of high value.

GOLD-FILLED use with any good gems.

VERMEIL (STERLING SILVER PLATED WITH GOLD) use with modest-value gems.

NIOBIUM (HYPO-ALLERGENIC METAL) use if you have an allergic reaction to silver.

SILVER (STERLING OR BETTER) use with gems of good quality.

PLATED BASE METAL use only with the very cheapest materials

STYLES OF CLASPS

- Hook-and-eye
- Fishhook
- Box
- Toggle
- Lobster claw
- Spring ring
- Sliding

FINDINGS FOR EARRINGS
EARWIRES

Earrings for pierced ears use earwires designed to fit through the pierced hole. Other earrings use earwires that clamp on to the earlobe with a clip or a screw. Earwires for pierced ears should always be of good quality and made from material that does not cause an allergic reaction.

FINDINGS COMMON TO BOTH EARRINGS AND NECKLACES
HEADPINS AND EYEPINS

These are simple pieces of straight wire on which you thread your beads. The "head" or "eye" at one end keeps the beads from falling off, and the other end is attached to the beading wire, chain, or earwire.

JUMP RINGS, SPLIT RINGS, AND PLAIN RINGS

These findings are often used for linking parts of necklaces and earrings. A jump ring is a simple metal loop that can be opened and closed by twisting. A split ring cannot be opened, but the item to be connected can be slipped onto it by feeding the item around the split in the side of the ring. (Split rings are just miniature versions of the metal rings on key chains.) A plain ring is one that cannot be opened because the ends are soldered together.

FINDINGS KEY

Following Pages

1. Gold-Filled Shepherd's Hook Earwire (left) "Add-On" Earwire (right)
2. Silver and Gold-Filled Crimp Beads
3. Silver Bead Caps
4. Silver Leverback Earwire (left) Earwire with Ball (right)
5. Silver Bead Caps
6. Silver and Gold-Filled Crimp Covers
7. Antiqued Silver Bead Caps
8. Silver and Gold-Filled Basket Bead Tips
9. Vermeil Headpins with Ball Tip
10. Gold-Filled Headpins
11. Silver and Gold-Filled Eyepin
12. Silver and Gold-Filled Rings
13. Silver Jump Rings
14. Silver and Vermeil Headpins with Ball Tip
15. Gold-Filled Lobster Clasp
16. Silver and Marcasite Toggle Clasp
17. Vermeil Lobster Clasp
18. Silver Box Clasp
19. Silver and Marcasite Toggle Clasp
20. Gold-Filled Box Clasp
21. Gold-Filled Box Clasp
22. Gold-Filled Lobster Clasp
23. Vermeil Toggle Clasp
24. "Stardust" Silver Toggle Clasp
25. Vermeil Lobster Clasp
26. Silver Hook-and-Eye Clasp
27. Silver Toggle Clasp
28. Vermeil Toggle Clasp
29. Silver Hook-and-Eye Clasp
30. Gold-Filled Three-Strand Sliding Clasp
31. Silver Hook-and-Eye Clasp
32. Gold-Filled Spring Ring Clasp
33. Silver Toggle Clasp

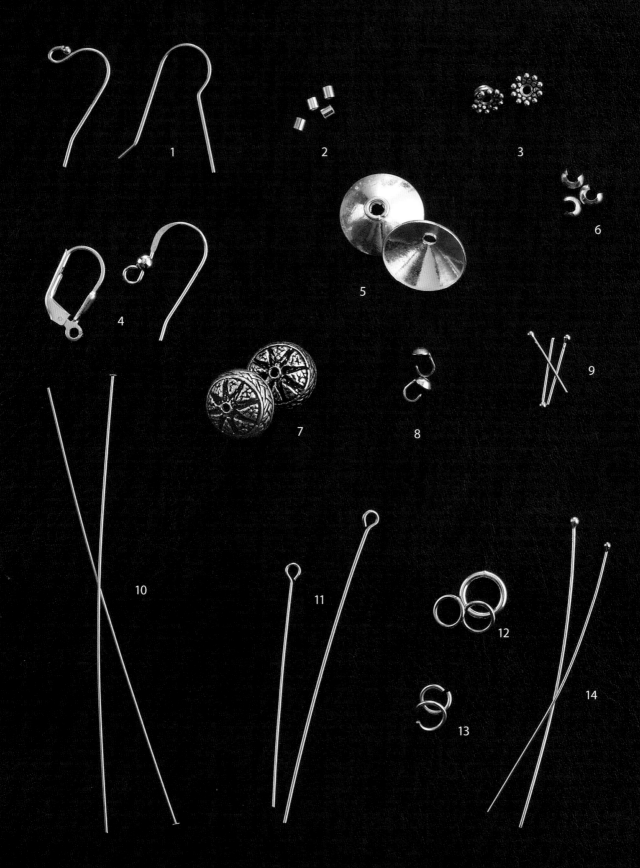

1

2

3

4

5

6

7

8

9

10

11

12

13

14

15

16

17

18

19

20

21

22

23

24

25

26

27

28

29

30

31

32

33

designing with gemstones

MAKING JEWELRY
WITH GEMSTONE BEADS

Making necklaces and earrings is simplicity itself. Although you still have to turn to the professional jeweler for setting rings and casting metals, you can master the basic techniques of stringing beads and bending wire in an evening. Combine these simple skills with a few inexpensive tools, add the basic ingredients of beads and findings, and you are ready to start making your own jewelry. Don't be intimidated! Compared with producing a decent meal, making a piece of jewelry is child's play—it requires fewer tools, and there are no dishes to wash up!

Every necklace or pair of earrings begins with the design. Although it is perfectly possible to throw random beads on a string, the results are unlikely to bring satisfaction. My own view of jewelry design begins with a simple premise: "The purpose of any body decoration is to enhance the look of the wearer." I consider whether the design goes well with the wearer's face, with the clothes she wears, with the mood she is in, and with the impression she wishes to make. Some designers might take the approach that the body is just a convenient frame to exhibit an interesting object, but if you are making jewelry for yourself I have little doubt you are sympathetic to the view that the jewels are there to make you look good, not the other way round. Although the jewelry in this book is in every way "contemporary," it uses "classic" design concepts—styles and materials that consistently return to the forefront of fashion and that have a proven record of making their owners feel they are wearing the "right stuff."

Because gemstone beads are, for the most part, natural stone, variation in color and quality is inherent. Even when you follow the design instructions to replicate the jewelry in this book, your components are unlikely to be exactly the same, and this gives your jewelry a unique look. Don't be shy about substituting other gemstones or colors for the ones in the illustrations. You should think of the instructions more like cooking recipes, where even small changes of ingredients can create a different but delightful flavor. Whether through desire to express your taste or a lack of access to the precise "ingredients," you should not hesitate to experiment with other materials to create your own unique "dish." Making these designs is, after all, even more rewarding if they include a dash of your own good judgment.

SUBSTITUTING FOR ECONOMY

Because there are such large price differences between gemstones, you should note that all these designs can be adapted to a lower budget by simply substituting a lower-price gemstone. For example, you can achieve a similar design for Simply Pink (page 42) using rose quartz instead of rhodochrosite. Any of the turquoise designs could be accomplished using stabilized turquoise, and cubic zirconia rondels could stand in for tourmaline. Choose a gemstone that is beautiful in your eyes but doesn't break your bank account.

If this book is your first introduction to making bead jewelry, you should start by browsing through the designs and choosing one that seems relatively easy to make. Then read the section "Jewelry Making Supplies" (page 22) for guidance on what tools to acquire, and the first page of "Basic Jewelry Making" (page 125) for useful tips. The rest of that chapter contains the instructions about stringing, attaching clasps, wrapping wire, working with earring findings and other information you need to make the designs in this book. Read the Jewelry Techniques chapter carefully, but note that these techniques are best learned through actual practice. When you feel comfortable, jump in and get started. As with all crafts, the only way to master the art of jewelry making is by actually doing it. It is my hope that after you have made a few of the designs in this book, you use your skills and your own design sense to purposely introduce variation and start creating entirely new designs of your own.

Whether substituting ingredients or planning a whole new design, you should follow these basic guidelines:

1. Do not mix inappropriate materials. Although it is obvious that you would not mix plastic beads with rubies or base metal with diamonds, the rule can quickly enter the gray area of subjective opinion.

2. No matter what they actually cost, never use materials that look cheap. They simply make the good look bad.

3. Use materials that have a fashion life span of decades rather than weeks. Today's fad is tomorrow's toast.

Unless otherwise stated, the necklace materials and instructions in this book are for 16-inch necklaces, the so-called "standard" short length. If this length does not suit you, adjust it by adding or subtracting from the materials and adjusting the pattern accordingly.

DESIGNING FOR YOU

When you are making jewelry for yourself or for friends or family, you have the opportunity to create something custom-built. You can do this by matching the colors with favorite clothes, to skin and hair tones, or to a preference for one shade or another. But you should also consider size. Bigger necks and busts obviously call for longer necklaces, but the size of the actual beads can be just as important. In designing commissioned pieces, my first thoughts are always to the shape of the client. The more delicate the bone structure and more petite her size, the more delicate should be the jewelry.

Although fashion and mood will dictate overall bead sizes, the general rule that "bigger women need bigger beads" is usually proved right, even if sometimes by its exceptions. Although there might be greater room for maneuver, size in jewelry is as important as size in clothing. No piece should either overwhelm or be overwhelmed by the body that wears it. In jewelry design the goal is harmony, not competition.

A ROPE OF GEMS

THE PROBLEM WITH LONG GEMSTONE NECKLACES IS THAT THEY USE A LOT OF GEMS AND CAN BECOME EXPENSIVE. ONE SOLUTION IS TO USE VERY SMALL BEADS, AND ANOTHER IS TO USE SPACER BEADS. IN THIS ROPE-LENGTH NECKLACE, I HAVE USED BOTH STRATEGIES BUT HAVE ALSO SCATTERED LARGER CITRINE BEADS ALONG THE STRAND TO CREATE MORE IMPACT. THE COLOR CHOICES ARE IMPORTANT BECAUSE THE OVERALL IMPRESSION SHOULD BE OF GEMSTONE AND GOLD ALONE. RATHER THAN ACTING AS SPACERS, THE BRONZE CHARLOTTE BEADS BLEND IN AND STRETCH OUT THE GEMSTONES. ALTHOUGH THE COLOR OF THESE TINY BEADS IS DARK, THE REFLECTIONS FROM THEIR IRIDESCENT SURFACES MIMIC THOSE FROM THE GOLD CHARLOTTES AND THE GEMSTONE BEADS.

1. Thread a crimp on the beading wire. Pass the wire through the ring of the clasp and back through the crimp. Make sure that the beading wire is tight around the ring and squeeze the crimp shut. Thread on a 2mm gold bead so that it fits over the tail of the wire and cut off any excess.

2. Start by adding a few charlotte beads, then a 3mm gemstone, a few more charlottes, and another 3mm gemstone. Continue in this manner, using the Note for help in balancing the random design. After about 1" add a vermeil daisy bead, an 8mm citrine bead, and another daisy before continuing with the random assortment of charlottes and 3mm gemstones.

3. Add another daisy, citrine, daisy combination after another 2". Continue the random charlotte and 3mm gem assortment, spacing the daisy, citrine, daisy combinations at intervals of approximately 3", 4", 3.5", 4", 1.5", 4.5", 3.5", 4", 2", 4", 1.5", 4", 3.5", 3, 4", 1.5", and 3".

4. Add the remaining charlottes and 3mm gems, then a 2mm gold bead, and the crimp. Bring the beading wire through the soldered ring and back through the crimp and round bead. Tighten the wire to eliminate spaces between the beads, close the crimp, and snip any excess wire. Add the crimp covers.

TOOLS
Wire Cutters, Crimping Pliers

MATERIALS (FOR A 21" NECKLACE)
19 8mm faceted round citrine beads

1 16" strand of 3mm faceted Tundra Sapphire* rondels

12 of size 15 gold-plated charlotte beads

36 of size 15 iridescent bronze charlotte beads

38 4mm vermeil daisy spacer beads

2 2mm hollow gold-filled round beads

1 gold-filled soldered ring

1 gold-filled spring ring clasp

2 gold-filled crimp beads

2 gold-filled crimp bead covers

76" of beading wire

*TUNDRA SAPPHIRE is a trade name for a particular color blend of gemstones, which are more likely to be garnets or other gemstones than actual sapphires. The effect is appealing, however, and the name has proven popular. You can use any multicolor strand of gemstones that pleases you.

NOTE
All the beads are added to the wire in a random pattern, except for the daisy spacers, which are used on either side of the citrine beads. In order to avoid ending up with an imbalance toward the end of the strand, check every 12" or so that you are using the right proportion of each type of bead. If you lay the temporary strands of beads out beside each other, it helps you judge whether you are using them at the same rate. For guidance, use the photograph of the necklace.

TRIANGULAR TOURMALINE NECKLACE

TOURMALINE IS TRIGONAL, WHICH MEANS THAT ITS LONG CRYSTALS HAVE A TRIANGULAR CROSS SECTION. TO MAKE THESE LOVELY AND UNUSUAL BEADS, THE CUTTER HAS TAKEN ADVANTAGE OF THE NATURAL SHAPE AND ADDED LONG FACETS THE LENGTH OF THE CRYSTAL THAT PROVIDE AN INTRIGUING REFLECTIVE PATTERN. BECAUSE OF ITS MANY COLORS, TOURMALINE CAN TAKE ON VARIOUS PERSONALITIES. THIS GREEN-BLUE COMBINATION IS QUIETLY ELEGANT, DISPLAYING THE OBVIOUS RICHNESS OF JEWELS IN A DISCREETLY UNDERSTATED FASHION.

IF THE TEMPORARY STRAND OF TOURMALINE IS ARRANGED IN A PLEASING MANNER, YOU CAN PLACE THE TOURMALINE BEADS IN THE ORDER THEY COME OFF THAT STRAND. IF NOT, THEN LAY OUT THE BEADS IN A LINE AND ARRANGE THEM HOW YOU WISH. PUT THE MOST IMPRESSIVE BEADS TOWARD THE CENTER AND THE LESS STRIKING ONES AT THE ENDS, WHERE THEY ARE HIDDEN BEHIND THE NECK.

1. Start the necklace by threading on a crimp. Pass the beading wire through the ring of one half of the clasp and back through the crimp. Make sure that the beading wire is tight around the ring and squeeze the crimp shut.

2. Thread on a 2mm gold bead so that it fits over the tail of the wire. Cut away the excess tail.

3. Add a pearl, a daisy spacer bead, a tourmaline bead, and another daisy spacer. Repeat this pattern 39 times or until the necklace has reached the length you desire.

4. Add a final pearl, the 2mm gold bead, and a crimp. Bring the beading wire through the ring of the other side of the clasp and back through the crimp and the gold bead. Tighten the necklace so that there are no spaces between the beads. Close the crimp and snip off any remaining beading wire. Add the crimp covers.

TOOLS
Wire Cutters, Crimping Pliers

MATERIALS

1   12" strand of triangular tourmaline beads approximately 7mm in diameter (the beads vary in length). Note: These strands often come in 14" lengths, allowing some beads to be left over for earrings.

41   2.5mm pearls (or one more than the number of tourmaline beads)

80   3mm 18 karat gold daisy spacer beads (or twice the number of tourmaline beads)

2   2mm hollow gold-filled round beads

1   18 karat gold hook-and-eye clasp

2   gold-filled crimp beads

2   gold-filled crimp bead covers

20"   of beading wire (gold color is preferable)

MOSS AQUAMARINE BRACELET

MOSS AQUAMARINE, OR "AQUA" FOR SHORT, IS REALLY JUST A PRETTY TRADE NAME FOR A QUALITY OF AQUAMARINE THAT HAS A LOT OF INCLUSIONS. ALTHOUGH LACK OF CLARITY GREATLY REDUCES THE PRICE OF AQUAMARINE, IT DOES NOT NECESSARILY LESSEN ITS ATTRACTIVENESS, AND IT CAN MAKE LARGER STONES QUITE AFFORDABLE. THE CLOUDY NATURE AND SUBTLE COLORS OF THESE FACETED NUGGETS MAKES THEM IDEAL CANDIDATES FOR JEWELRY OF UNDERSTATED ELEGANCE.

1. Start the bracelet by threading on a crimp. Pass the beading wire through the ring of one half of the clasp and back through the crimp. Make sure that the beading wire is tight around the ring and squeeze the crimp shut.

2. Thread on a 3mm round silver bead and a Thai silver chip so that they fit over the tail of the wire and cut away any excess.

3. Add a moss aqua nugget, a 2.5mm silver round, a Thai silver chip, and another 2.5mm silver round. Repeat this step 8 more times.

4. Add a Thai silver chip, a 3mm round bead, and a crimp. Bring the beading wire through the ring of the other side of the clasp and back through the crimp and the round bead. Tighten the bracelet so that there are no spaces between the beads, close the crimp, and snip off any remaining wire. Add the crimp covers.

5. Make the dangle by adding to the headpin a Thai silver chip, a 2.5mm silver round bead, a moss aqua nugget, a silver round, another Thai silver chip, and the last 2.5mm silver round. Cut the headpin 5/8" above the last bead and start a wrapped loop. Attach it to the loop of the clasp ring and finish it off with several turns around the base.

TOOLS

Crimping Pliers, Flat-Nosed Pliers, Wire Cutters, Round-Nosed Pliers

MATERIALS

10	12mm by 10mm (approximately) faceted moss aquamarine nuggets
12	1mm by 4mm (approximately) Thai silver chips
20	2.5mm hollow silver round beads
2	3mm hollow silver round beads
1	2" silver headpin with ball tip
2	silver crimp beads
2	silver crimp bead covers
1	silver toggle clasp
10"	of beading wire

PERUVIAN OPAL NECKLACE

SOME GEMSTONES CAN BE QUITE ATTRACTIVE WHEN THEY ARE IRREGULARLY FACETED. ALTHOUGH THESE PERUVIAN OPALS ARE CUT AND POLISHED, THEY RETAIN A FEELING OF ROUGH STONE, AS IF THESE HAD BEEN FOUND AS NATURAL SHAPES. THIS GIVES THEM A WARM, ORGANIC FEEL THAT GOES WELL WITH THE INHERENT COLOR VARIATION OF THE STONE.

1. First you need to make the loop of beads that holds your centerpiece pendant. Note that the number of black onyx beads you use will depend on the size of the hole in the centerpiece bead. If it is bigger than 2mm, then the onyx beads will fit through the hole and you will need more. If only the wire fits through the hole, you will need fewer onyx beads. Decide which surface of your centerpiece you want to be in front and pass the beading wire through from that direction. Thread on 2 onyx beads and a crimp. Continue adding onyx beads (about 12) until when you take the beading wire back through the front of the centerpiece, the loop is entirely covered. The loop should not be tight around the rim of the pendant—you need a space of 4mm to 5mm to allow room to attach it to the main strand. Bring the beading wire through the pendant again and through the first 2 beads and the crimp. Tighten the wire so that all the beads are snug against each other. The crimp should now lay hidden at the back of the pendant and the loop should not be too tight or too loose. If there is a problem, bring the wire back and add or subtract beads as necessary. When you're satisfied with the appearance, close the crimp and snip away the rest of the wire. Add the crimp cover.

2. Using the rest of the beading wire, start the necklace by threading on a crimp. Pass the beading wire through the ring of one half of the clasp and back through the crimp. Make sure that the beading wire is tight around the ring and squeeze the crimp shut. Add a round gold bead so that it covers the tail of the wire and cut away any excess. Then add 5 onyx beads.

3. Add a Peruvian opal chip and an onyx bead. Repeat this pattern 32 times. Pass the wire through the loop of the pendant. Check the necklace against your neck to make sure the length is right.

TOOLS
Crimping Pliers, Wire Cutters

MATERIALS

16"	of Peruvian opal chips approximately 8mm to 10mm wide (half a 32" strand)
1	Peruvian opal centerpiece pendant bead approximately 40mm by 30mm
90	2mm round black onyx beads
2	3mm seamless hollow gold-filled round beads
3	gold-filled crimp beads
3	gold-filled crimp bead covers
1	vermeil toggle clasp
24"	of beading wire

4. Add an onyx and a Peruvian opal bead. Repeat this pattern 32 times. Check to make sure that the sides of the necklace are equal in length. If they are not, change the last few chips to thicker or thinner ones to make the sides even.

5. Add 5 onyx beads, a gold bead, and a crimp. Pass the wire through the loop of the other half of the clasp and back through the crimp and the gold bead. Make sure that the beading wire is tight around the ring and squeeze the crimp shut. Cut away the excess wire and add the crimp covers.

PICTURE JASPER CENTERPIECE NECKLACE

SOME STONES DON'T DEPEND ON REFLECTIVITY, LUSTER, OR OPTICAL EFFECT FOR THEIR VALUE, BUT ON FASCINATING PATTERNS AND ARRANGEMENTS OF COLOR. PICTURE, OR LANDSCAPE, JASPER IS A CLASSIC EXAMPLE OF THESE KINDS OF STONES.

THIS IS AN UNUSUAL CONSTRUCTION BECAUSE THE NECKLACE IS MADE IN TWO HALVES THAT ARE THEN JOINED BY THE CENTERPIECE. THE STRANDS OF CHARLOTTES ATTACHING EACH HALF OF THE NECKLACE ARE SECURED BY CRIMPS THAT ARE HIDDEN BEHIND THE CENTERPIECE.

1. Start one side of the necklace by threading on a crimp. Pass the beading wire through the ring of one half of the clasp and back through the crimp. Make sure that the beading wire is tight around the ring and squeeze the crimp shut. Add a gold round bead so that it covers the tail and cut off any excess wire.

2. Thread on 11 charlotte beads and a round jasper bead. Add 3 charlotte beads and a jasper bead. Repeat this pattern 15 times. Add a crimp bead and jasper bead. Thread on 18 charlotte beads and bring the beading wire back through the hole of the last jasper bead, the crimp, and the next jasper bead. Tighten the wire to eliminate spaces between the beads. Once the charlotte beads form a nicely shaped loop at the end of the strand, close the crimp and cut the excess beading wire.

3. Make a second strand on the other half of the clasp following steps 1 and 2.

4. To make the loops, use a bead stopper or a binder clip to stop the beads from falling off the beading wire, then add a crimp and approximately 2" of charlottes to the beading wire. (Leave at least 2" of beading wire on the other side of the crimp and clip so you have something to grip when you finish.) Select the side of the centerpiece you wish to be the front and position the crimp at the back. Pass the wire with the charlottes through one of the centerpiece holes and around the front side of the disc. Pass it through the beaded loop at the end of one of the strands. Pass it around to the back of the centerpiece again and through the hole. Adjust the number of charlottes to keep the crimp positioned

TOOLS
Wire Cutters, Crimping Pliers, Bead Stopper or Binder Clip

MATERIALS (FOR A 22" NECKLACE)
- 36   10mm round green jasper beads
- 1   50mm picture jasper disc (also known as landscape jasper) with two holes (button drilled)
- 14" of size 13 copper-plated charlotte beads
- 2   3mm seamless hollow gold-filled round beads
- 1   vermeil toggle clasp
- 6   gold-filled crimp beads
- 6   gold-filled crimp bead covers
- 32" of beading wire

halfway between the hole and the edge of the disc. Once the wire is back through the hole, add more charlottes and bring the wire around the side of the disc, through the beaded loop, and back through the crimp. Tighten the wire to make sure all the wire is covered and the bands are snug around the edges of the disc. Make sure the loop of the strand sits at the front of the disc. Close the crimp and cut away the remaining wire.

5. Repeat step 4 to attach the other half of the necklace to the other side of the disc. Add the crimp covers.

SIMPLY PINK

THE NATURAL COLOR OF RHODOCHROSITE IS A DELIGHTFUL
SHADE OF PINK. ALTHOUGH MOST COMMONLY FOUND BANDED,
SOME, SUCH AS THIS BEAUTIFUL AMERICAN CRYSTAL, ARE
DISCOVERED IN PURE PINK. FOR A STRAND OF GEMS AS
STUNNING AS THIS, I SOMETIMES PREFER TO TREAT THEM AS I
WOULD EXPENSIVE PEARLS AND STRING THEM ON SILK. NO
OTHER STRINGING MATERIAL IS AS FLEXIBLE AND ALLOWS THEM
TO FLOW AROUND THE NECK IN QUITE THE SAME WAY. THE BEADS
ARE SO LOVELY THAT ONLY THE SIMPLEST TOUCH, SUCH AS THESE
TINY GOLD BEAD CAPS, IS REQUIRED TO DISPLAY THEM TO THEIR
BEST ADVANTAGE. THE SAME TREATMENT WORKS EQUALLY WELL
FOR ANY OTHER SMOOTHLY POLISHED, FINE GEMSTONE BEADS.

1. Read the instructions in Getting Knotted (page 128) for stringing
   on silk thread and clamshell bead tips. In this design, however,
   you are not going to knot between every bead, only
   at the beginning and end of the necklace. Start by threading
   a beading needle and making a knot at the end of the doubled
   thread. Following the instructions in Jewelry Techniques (page
   130), add one of the bead tips. Once the bead tip is secure, add a
   4mm gold bead.

2. Now add a 2mm gold bead, a bead cap, a gemstone bead, and
   another bead cap. Make sure the bead caps have their concave
   sides toward the gemstone beads. Repeat this pattern another
   39 times or until the necklace is the length you wish.

3. Add one more 2mm gold bead and the 4mm gold bead. Tighten
   the cord and make sure all the beads and bead caps fit snugly
   together. Make a knot and, using your awl, tighten it firmly
   against the last bead, then the other bead tip. Attach the clasp
   to the bead tips.

TOOLS
Beading Needle, Awl, Scissors,
Flat-Nosed Pliers

MATERIALS
40	8mm round rhodochrosite beads
80	4.5mm gold-filled bead caps
2	4mm gold-filled seamless hollow round beads
41	2mm gold-filled hollow round beads
2	gold-filled clamshell bead tips
1	gold-filled fishhook clasp
2	yards of silk thread, size F

RUBIES AND ROSE QUARTZ NECKLACE

THE IMPRECISE LABELING OF STONES AS "PRECIOUS" OR "SEMIPRECIOUS" IS CONFUSED BY THE FACT THAT SOME STONES, SUCH AS ROSE QUARTZ, WHICH SEEM TO FIT SO NEATLY INTO THE "SEMIPRECIOUS" REALM, ALSO HAVE "GEM-QUALITY" VERSIONS. ALTHOUGH THIS LABEL ALSO IS SUBJECTIVE, IT DOES EXPRESS THE REAL DIFFERENCE BETWEEN THE APPEARANCE AND THE COST OF ORDINARY ROSE QUARTZ AND A STONE OF EXCEPTIONAL CLARITY, SUCH AS THE CENTERPIECE OF THIS NECKLACE. WITH LITTLE RECTANGULAR FACETS, THE CUTTER HAS WORKED AROUND A FRACTURE IN THIS DROP, TURNING THE FLAW TO AN ADVANTAGE AND CREATING FLASHES OF INTERNAL FIRE. ALTHOUGH IT IS THE RUBIES THAT ARE DECIDEDLY "PRECIOUS," IT IS THE ROSE QUARTZ THAT IS THE OBVIOUS JEWEL.

1. First make the pendant. Add a 2.5mm gold bead to the headpin, then the rose quartz drop and another 2.5mm gold bead. Cut the headpin about ⅝" above the bead and make a wire-wrapped loop.

2. Start the necklace by threading on a crimp. Pass the beading wire through the ring of one half of the clasp and back through the crimp. Make sure that the beading wire is tight around the ring and squeeze the crimp shut. Add a 2.5mm round gold bead so that it covers the tail of the wire and cut away any excess.

3. Add 2 more gold beads. Now, add half of the strand of ruby beads followed by another gold bead. Pass the beading wire through the loop of the pendant, add another gold bead and then the rest of the ruby beads. Hold the necklace up to check that the rubies on either side are of equal length.

4. Add the last 3 gold round beads and a crimp. Bring the beading wire through the ring of the other side of the clasp and back through the crimp and the last 2 beads. Now tighten the necklace so that there are no spaces between the beads, close the crimp, and snip off any remaining beading wire. Add the crimp covers.

TOOLS
Wire Cutters, Crimping Pliers,
Round-Nosed Pliers

MATERIALS

1	15" strand of 3mm by 4mm faceted ruby rondel beads
1	27mm by 17mm faceted rose quartz teardrop bead
10	2.5mm hollow gold-filled round beads
1	2" vermeil headpin with ball tip
1	vermeil hook-and-eye clasp
2	gold-filled crimp beads
2	gold-filled crimp bead covers
20"	of beading wire (preferably gold color)

JADE AND AQUAMARINE NECKLACE

MANY GEMSTONES HAVE A "PRECIOUS" QUALITY AND A "COMMON" VARIETY THAT, AS IN THE CASE OF OPAL, CAN SOMETIMES LOOK DIFFERENT ENOUGH TO APPEAR TO BE A DIFFERENT STONE. SUCH IS THE CASE WITH THESE LARGE AQUAMARINE BEADS. ALMOST COMPLETELY OPAQUE AND MOTTLED IN COLOR, THEY SEEM UTTERLY REMOTE FROM THEIR PRECIOUS COUSIN, BUT STILL DELIGHTFUL WITH THEIR OWN DISTINCTIVE CHARM AND SOFT COLOR TONES. THE SMALL JADE DISCS COMPLEMENT THE AQUAMARINE AND EMPHASIZE THE WARMTH OF NATURAL ORGANIC COLORS.

1. Start the necklace by threading on a crimp. Pass the beading wire through the ring of one half of the clasp and back through the crimp. Make sure that the beading wire is tight around the ring and squeeze the crimp shut.

2. Thread on 3 gold round beads so that they fit over the tail of the wire and cut away any excess.

3. Add a daisy spacer bead, 3 jade discs, a daisy, a gold round bead, another daisy, an aquamarine bead, another daisy, and a gold round bead. Repeat this pattern 16 more times.

4. Add a daisy, 3 jade discs, another daisy, 3 gold round beads, and a crimp. Bring the beading wire through the ring of the other side of the clasp and back through the crimp and round beads. Tighten the necklace so that there are no spaces between the beads, close the crimp, and snip off any remaining beading wire. Add the crimp covers.

TOOLS
Wire Cutters, Crimping Pliers

MATERIALS

17	14mm round aquamarine beads
54	1.5mm by 8mm jade disc beads
70	4mm vermeil star-shaped daisy spacer beads
40	2.5mm hollow gold-filled round beads
1	large (25mm) vermeil toggle clasp
2	gold-filled crimp beads
2	gold-filled crimp bead covers
22"	of beading wire

LABRADORITE BRIOLETTES NECKLACE

I LOVE HEART-SHAPED BRIOLETTES. THEIR FLATTENED FACETED SURFACE CREATES A BROAD REFLECTIVE AREA, MAKING THE MOST PROFITABLE USE OF THE GEMSTONE. THE CURVING, GOLD-FILLED TUBES NOT ONLY CREATE A SIMPLE ELEGANCE, BUT THEY MAKE IT EASY TO CONSTRUCT A LONG NECKLACE QUICKLY. THE DESIGN IS ALSO FLEXIBLE. HERE, I HAVE USED SOME LOVELY LABRADORITE STONES AND MATCHED THEIR BLUE-GRAY IRIDESCENCE WITH THE TINIEST OF AQUAMARINE ROUND BEADS TO FRAME EACH CLUSTER OF BRIOLETTES. BUT YOU CAN USE WHATEVER GEMSTONE PLEASES YOU AND CHANGE THE GOLD-FILLED TUBES TO SILVER IF YOU WISH.

1. Thread a crimp on the beading wire. Pass the wire through the ring of the clasp and back through the crimp. Make sure that the beading wire is tight around the ring and squeeze the crimp shut. Thread on two 2mm gold beads so that they fit over the tail of the wire and cut off any excess wire.

2. Thread on a 2mm aquamarine bead, a 20mm tube, another aquamarine bead, followed by a 2mm gold bead, a 4mm daisy spacer bead, a labradorite briolette, another daisy, a briolette, daisy, briolette, daisy, and gold bead. Repeat this pattern 10 times.

3. Now add an aquamarine bead, a gold tube, another aquamarine bead, two 2mm gold beads, and a crimp. Bring the beading wire through the ring of the other side of the clasp and back through the crimp and its adjacent round gold bead. Before tightening the necklace, lay it out and make sure that all the briolettes at the center of each cluster fall on the opposite side to the briolettes at the ends. Carefully tighten the necklace so that all the beads are snugly together, close the crimp, and snip off any remaining beading wire. Add the crimp covers.

TOOLS
Wire Cutters, Crimping Pliers

MATERIALS (FOR A 20" NECKLACE)

33 8mm by 8mm faceted labradorite heart-shaped beads (briolettes)

24 2mm aquamarine round beads

12 20mm gold-filled tube beads bent to form a shallow wave

44 4mm vermeil daisy spacer beads

26 2mm hollow gold-filled round beads

1 7mm gold-filled ring

1 7mm gold-filled spring ring clasp

2 gold-filled crimp beads

2 gold-filled crimp bead covers

26" of beading wire

TURQUOISE AND HESSONITE NECKLACE

THESE TUMBLED DROPS OF CHINESE TURQUOISE HAVE A BEAUTIFUL COLOR AND FORM AN EXTRAVAGANT FRAME FOR THE DRAMATIC PATTERNS OF THE CENTRAL PENDANT.

ALTHOUGH SOME TURQUOISE IS PURE BLUE, MOST IS INTERSPERSED WITH BROWN OR BLACK VEINS OF OTHER MINERALS, A FEATURE THAT OFTEN GIVES IT A MORE INTERESTING CHARACTER. HESSONITE, A TYPE OF GARNET, HAS A RICH MAPLE SYRUP HUE WHICH PICKS UP AND EMPHASIZES THE HONEY BROWN VEINS OF THE TURQUOISE.

1. First make the pendant loop. Decide which is the back of the pendant bead. Pass the beading wire through the front of the pendant, then add a hessonite bead and a crimp so that they are at the back of the pendant. Add a hessonite and a daisy. Repeat 5 times and add the final hessonite. Pass the wire back through the front of the pendant, the hessonite bead, the crimp, and the next hessonite bead. Now tighten the loop so that all the beads are snug. There must be about 3mm to 4mm of space between the top of the pendant bead and the top of the loop.

2. Thread a crimp on the beading wire. Pass the wire through the ring of one half of the clasp and back through the crimp. Make sure that the beading wire is tight around the ring and squeeze the crimp shut. Thread on three 3mm silver beads so that they fit over the tail of the wire and cut off any excess.

3. Thread on a hessonite bead, a silver daisy, a turquoise bead, and another daisy.

4. Add a hessonite, daisy, turquoise, daisy, turquoise, daisy, turquoise, daisy, hessonite, daisy, turquoise, daisy, turquoise, daisy, turquoise, daisy, turquoise daisy, turquoise, and daisy. Repeat this pattern 2 more times. Then add a hessonite, daisy, turquoise, daisy, turquoise, daisy, turquoise, daisy, hessonite, 3 daisies, and a 3mm silver round bead.

5. Add the pendant loop, then reverse the directions in steps 3 and 4 to make the other half of the necklace a mirror image of the first. Add 3 round silver beads and the crimp. Bring the beading wire through the ring of the other side of the clasp and back through the crimp and silver round bead. Tighten the necklace so that there are no spaces between the beads, close the crimp, and snip off any remaining beading wire. Add the crimp covers.

TOOLS
Wire Cutters, Crimping Pliers

MATERIALS
56 top-drilled Chinese turquoise tumbled drops approximately 15mm to 20mm in length

1 25mm by 48mm Chinese turquoise pendant bead

25 3mm hessonite round beads

83 4mm silver daisy spacer beads

8 3mm seamless hollow silver round beads

1 silver toggle clasp

3 silver crimp beads

2 silver crimp bead covers

24" of beading wire

NOTE
Depending on where the hole is drilled in your pendant bead, you may need more or fewer hessonite and daisy beads to make the pendant loop.

BLACK ONYX CHOKER

ALTHOUGH THE MATTE SURFACE OF THESE LARGE BLACK ONYX
SHARDS IS PROPERLY DESCRIBED AS "DULL," THEY CAN BE USED
TO SPECTACULAR EFFECT IN A NECKLACE. UNLIKE THE SHARDS OF
KYANITE CRYSTALS ON PAGE 84, THESE ARE PURPOSELY CUT TO
ACHIEVE A DRAMATIC EFFECT. THE LAPIS LAZULI PROVIDES A
SUBTLE CONTRAST AND THE LITTLE GOLD SPACERS ADD A
DELICATE TOUCH OF GLITTER.

1. Start the necklace by threading on a crimp. Pass the beading
   wire through the ring of one half of the clasp and back through
   the crimp. Make sure that the beading wire is tight around the
   ring and squeeze the crimp shut.

2. Thread on a gold round bead so that it fits over the tail of the
   wire and cut away any excess. Then add a daisy spacer bead, a
   4mm lapis bead, a 6mm lapis bead, another 4mm lapis, a daisy
   spacer, and a black onyx shard. Repeat this pattern 12 times.

3. Add another daisy spacer bead, a 4mm lapis bead, a 6mm lapis
   bead, another 4mm lapis, a daisy spacer, a gold round bead, and
   a crimp. Bring the beading wire through the ring of the other
   side of the clasp and back through the crimp and round bead.
   Tighten the necklace so that there are no spaces between the
   beads, close the crimp, and snip off any remaining beading wire.
   Add the crimp covers.

TOOLS
Wire Cutters, Crimping Pliers

MATERIALS

13	10mm by 40mm to 50mm black onyx shards with a matte surface
14	6mm lapis lazuli round beads
28	4mm lapis lazuli round beads
28	4mm vermeil daisy spacer beads
2	3mm hollow seamless gold-filled round beads
1	vermeil toggle clasp
2	gold-filled crimp beads
2	gold-filled crimp bead covers
20"	of beading wire

CITRINE BRACELET

THE NATURAL COLOR OF CITRINE IS, AS THE NAME IMPLIES, LEMON YELLOW—AN ALMOST IMPOSSIBLE TONE FOR MANY WOMEN TO WEAR. BUT MOST CITRINE NOW ON THE MARKET IS IN ITS HEAT-TREATED FORM. THIS ENHANCEMENT ADDS A REDEEMING TINGE OF RED (MOST MODERN CITRINE IS ACTUALLY HEAT-TREATED AMETHYST, ANOTHER SILICON DIOXIDE QUARTZ THAT ADAPTS EASILY TO THE PREFERRED COLOR). ALTHOUGH HEAT TREATING GIVES CITRINE A LOVELY WARM GLOW, IT STILL HAS A DANGEROUS TENDENCY TOWARD ORANGE, SO I ALWAYS COMBINE IT WITH MORE MUTED COLORS TO SOFTEN THE EFFECT.

1. Start the bracelet by threading on a crimp. Pass the beading wire through the ring of one half of the clasp and back through the crimp. Make sure that the beading wire is tight around the ring and squeeze the crimp shut.

2. Thread on a 2.5mm round gold round bead so that it fits over the tail of the wire and cut away any excess.

3. Referring to the bead codes in the materials list, add beads as follows: G, C, P, C, D, A, D, C, Z, C, D, A, D, C, G, C, P, C, G, C, D, A, D, C, Z, C, D, A, D, C, G, C, P, C, Z, C, D, A, D, C, Z, D, A.

4. Reverse the order in step 3, beginning with D, to create the other half of the bracelet. Add the other 2.5mm gold bead and a crimp. Bring the beading wire through the ring of the other side of the clasp and back through the crimp and the round beads. Tighten the bracelet so that there are no spaces between the beads, close the crimp, and snip off any remaining wire. Add the crimp covers.

5. Make the dangle by adding a gold daisy, citrine, charlotte, zircon, garnet, and another charlotte to the headpin. Form the rest of the headpin into a wire-wrapped loop. Use the jump ring to attach the dangle to the ring of the clasp.

TOOLS
Crimping Pliers, Flat-Nosed Pliers, Wire Cutters, Round-Nosed Pliers

MATERIALS
12 5mm by 8mm faceted citrine rondel beads (A)

9 2mm by 4mm faceted natural zircon rondel beads (Z)

6 2mm by 4mm faceted peridot rondel beads (P)

9 3mm faceted garnet round beads (G)

23 4mm vermeil star daisy spacer beads (D)

32 size 15/0 gold-plated charlotte beads (C)

2 2.5mm hollow gold-filled round beads

1 4mm gold-filled jump ring

1 1¼" gold-filled headpin with ball tip

2 gold-filled crimp beads

2 gold-filled crimp bead covers

1 vermeil toggle clasp

10" of beading wire

NOTE
If there is any size variation in the citrine beads, reserve the largest for the central bead of the bracelet.

FIRE AGATE NECKLACE

AGATE, A BANDED FORM OF CHALCEDONY, COMES IN A VARIETY OF PATTERNS AND COLORS. FIRE AGATE FROM MEXICO AND ARIZONA IS ONE OF THE MOST INTERESTING FORMS BECAUSE IT HAS A DISTINCTIVE IRIDESCENT QUALITY CAUSED BY AN INTERNAL LAYER OF IRON OXIDE. THE LARGE PENDANT BEAD AT THE CENTER EMPHASIZES THE STRONG PATTERNING THAT IS THE LEADING CHARACTERISTIC OF THIS FAMILY OF GEMSTONES.

1. Start the necklace by threading on a crimp. Pass the beading wire through the ring of one half of the clasp and back through the crimp. Add a gold round bead so that it covers the tail of the beading wire, make sure that the wire is tight around the ring, squeeze the crimp shut, and cut away any excess tail.

2. Thread on a daisy spacer bead, a carnelian bead, another daisy, and an 8mm fire agate. Repeat this pattern 1 more time.

3. Add a daisy spacer, a 10mm fire agate, daisy, 8mm fire agate, daisy, carnelian, daisy, 8mm fire agate, daisy, carnelian, daisy, and 8mm fire agate. Repeat this pattern 2 times.

4. Add a daisy spacer, a 10mm fire agate, daisy, 8mm fire agate, daisy, carnelian, daisy, 8mm fire agate, and 3 daisy spacers.

5. Add the pendant bead and then the rest of your beads, reversing the instructions in steps 2 to 4 to create the other half of the necklace as a matching half of the first.

6. Add a round gold bead and a crimp. Bring the beading wire through the ring of the other side of the clasp and back through the crimp and the gold bead. Tighten the necklace so that there are no spaces between the beads. Close the crimp and snip off any remaining beading wire. Add the crimp covers.

TOOLS
Wire Cutters, Crimping Pliers

MATERIALS
1   40mm by 30mm top-drilled fire agate pendant bead

8   10mm fire agate round beads

26   8mm fire agate round beads

18   4mm carnelian round beads

58   4mm vermeil daisy spacer beads

2   3mm seamless hollow gold-filled round beads

1   vermeil toggle clasp

2   gold-filled crimp beads

2   gold-filled crimp bead covers

22"   of beading wire

PINK TOURMALINE WITH TOPAZ NECKLACE

GRADUATED STRANDS OF GEMSTONES ARE READILY AVAILABLE BECAUSE THEY ARE AFFORDABLE FOR CUSTOMERS AND CONVENIENT FOR GEMSTONE CUTTERS. BECAUSE THE SIZE OF A CUT GEM IS PARTLY DICTATED BY THE RAW MATERIAL, CUTTERS OFTEN END UP MAKING MANY DIFFERENT SIZES FROM THE ROUGH STONE. IN THIS DESIGN, GRADUATION HAS ALLOWED ME TO USE A FAIRLY LARGE CENTRAL BEAD. THE TOPAZ AND GOLD BEADS ECONOMICALLY SPACE OUT THE FAR MORE EXPENSIVE BRIOLETTES BUT MAINTAIN THE OVERALL IMPRESSION OF SERIOUS JEWELS!

1. Start the necklace by threading on a crimp. Pass the beading wire through the end link of one half of the clasp (or through the ring if your clasp doesn't have the chain links) and back through the crimp. Make sure that the beading wire is tight around the ring and squeeze the crimp shut.

2. Thread on 3 round gold beads so that they fit over the tail of the wire. If there is any excess tail, cut it away.

3. Add a topaz bead and a round gold bead. Repeat 4 times.

4. Add a daisy spacer bead, and the first of the tourmaline briolettes, then another daisy spacer, a topaz bead, a gold round, a topaz, a gold round, and another topaz. Repeat this pattern 32 times, taking care to add the briolettes in the order in which they come off the temporary strand.

5. Add another gold round bead, a topaz, a gold round, a topaz, 3 gold rounds, and a crimp. Hold the necklace around your neck to make sure of the length and to ensure that the largest briolette is well centered. Bring the beading wire through the end link of the other side of the clasp and back through the crimp and the gold beads (or as many of them as the wire will pass through easily). Tighten the necklace so there are no spaces between the beads, close the crimp, and snip off any remaining beading wire.

TOOLS
Wire Cutters, Crimping Pliers

MATERIALS

33 pink tourmaline faceted teardrops (briolettes) graduated in size from 8mm by 12mm to 4mm by 6.5mm (This strand was about 7" in length with little gold-plated spacer beads. If the graduated strand you buy has a smaller number of briolettes, you can deduct them from the ends of the necklace.)

106 2mm by 3mm blue topaz faceted rondels (approximately 9")

82 1.5mm round 18 karat gold beads (You could also substitute size 13/0 gold-plated charlotte beads.)

66 3mm 18 karat gold daisy spacer beads

1 18 karat gold toggle clasp with 4 chain links on either side (You can use a regular toggle clasp.)

2 gold-filled crimp beads

22" of beading wire (gold color is preferable)

NOTES
If the briolettes are already nicely graduated on the temporary strand, as they should be, leave them on the strand and remove them one by one as you add them to the necklace.

I have not used crimp covers on this necklace because 18 karat gold covers are not easily available. I prefer to leave the crimp, which is barely visible, exposed rather than add a larger element in a different karat gold.

GEMSTONE SAMPLER ROPE NECKLACE

AFTER YOU HAVE SPENT A WHILE MAKING JEWELRY, YOU FIND THAT YOU HAVE A GROWING NUMBER OF BEADS EITHER LEFT OVER FROM OTHER DESIGNS OR ACQUIRED WITHOUT A SPECIFIC PURPOSE, SIMPLY BECAUSE YOU LIKED THEM. THIS KIND OF NECKLACE IS A PERFECT WAY TO PUT ALL THOSE LONESOME BEADS TO GOOD USE. BY ITS VERY NATURE, THIS IS A DESIGN THAT YOU WON'T BE ABLE TO REPRODUCE EXACTLY AS PICTURED, BUT THE CONCEPT CAN GUIDE YOU IN DESIGNING YOUR OWN UNIQUE NECKLACE, COMPOSED OF THE BEADS YOU HAVE AVAILABLE. I HAVE LISTED THE MATERIALS I USED TO GIVE YOU SOME IDEA OF THE TYPES OF BEADS THAT MIGHT BE USED.

1. Thread a crimp on the beading wire. Pass the wire through the ring of one half of the clasp and back through the crimp. Make sure that the beading wire is tight around the ring and squeeze the crimp shut. Thread on a 3mm round silver bead so that it fits over the tail of the wire and cut off any excess.

2. Add your beads in a random fashion, checking for a pleasing balance as you go.

3. When you have used all of your beads or reached the length you desire, add a 3mm silver round and the crimp. Bring the beading wire through the ring of the other side of the clasp and back through the crimp and round bead. Tighten the necklace so that there are no spaces between the beads, close the crimp, and snip off any remaining beading wire. Add the crimp covers.

TOOLS
Wire Cutters, Crimping Pliers

MATERIALS (FOR A 52" ROPE NECKLACE)

125 assorted gemstone beads ranging in size from 2mm to 14mm (My selection includes garnet, apatite, morganite, blue lace agate, peridot, Swiss blue topaz, iolite, Peruvian opal, vesuvianite, turquoise, amethyst, zircon, carnelian, tourmaline, aventurine, kyanite, labradorite, lapis lazuli, pearls, and jade.)

30 2mm peridot faceted round beads

4" approximately of 1mm faceted Thai silver beads

1 20mm Thai silver "woven ball" bead

6 6mm Balinese silver beads

6 5mm silver bells

7 assorted silver bead caps

3 large silver beads

2 7mm silver rondels set with crystal

29 Thai silver tubes ranging from 10mm to 20mm in length

24 1mm silver twisted tubes

40 4mm silver daisy spacer beads

14 6mm coil spacer beads

83 2mm hollow silver round beads

24 2.5mm hollow silver round beads

18 3mm hollow silver round beads

1 silver spring ring clasp

2 silver crimp beads

2 silver crimp bead covers

56" of beading wire

NOTE
It's easier to balance the arrangement of beads on the wire rather than laying them out before stringing. Each 6" or so, check that the balance of beads looks pleasing. Because this is a clasped necklace, you can make it any length you like, depending on materials.

SUMMER COLORS NECKLACE

AS WITH CLOTHING, JEWELRY FASHIONS ARE OFTEN SEASONAL, AND COLOR MIXTURES ARE SOMETIMES DESCRIBED BY THE TIME OF THE YEAR THEY ARE MOST POPULAR. BRIGHT HUES ARE THOUGHT OF AS "SUMMERY," WHEREAS THE MORE SOMBER SHADES ARE CONSIDERED MORE APPROPRIATE FOR WINTER WEAR. THERE IS EVEN ONE GEMSTONE, "AUTUMN" TOURMALINE, THAT IS COMPLETELY DEFINED BY ITS SEASON. OF COURSE, THERE ARE NO HARD AND FAST RULES, AND THOSE FORTUNATE ENOUGH TO LIVE IN THE TROPICS AVOID THE ISSUE ALTOGETHER. BUT FOR THOSE WHO LIVE IN NORTHERN CLIMES, HERE IS A MIX OF GEMSTONES THAT HAVE A "SUMMER" ASPECT.

1. Start the necklace by threading on a crimp. Pass the beading wire through the ring of one half of the clasp and back through the crimp. Make sure that the beading wire is tight around the ring and squeeze the crimp shut.

2. Thread on a gold round bead so that it fits over the tail of the wire and cut away any excess. Then, referring to the bead codes in the materials list, add beads as follows: 5B, C, A, D, A, C, 3E, F, G, F, 3E, C, A, C, 3H, C, A, 3B, C, A, D, A, C, E, A, G, A, E, 3F, E, C, A, 3H, A, C, 3B, A, D, A, C, E, C, A, D, A, C, E, C, A, D, A, B, A, C, 3H, C, A, 3E, A, C, A, G, A, C, E, C, A, D, A, B, F, B, F, B, A. C, 3H, C, A, G, A, F, 3E, F, A, C.

3. Add the centerpiece pendant bead and continue the strand by reversing the order of the pattern in step 2.

4. After the final gold round bead, add a crimp. Bring the beading wire through the ring of the other side of the clasp and back through the crimp and round bead. Tighten the necklace so that there are no spaces between the beads, close the crimp, and snip off any remaining beading wire. Add the crimp covers.

TOOLS
Wire Cutters, Crimping Pliers

MATERIALS

1	16mm by 20mm citrine faceted pendant bead
24	6mm by 8mm iolite faceted drops (H)
8	6mm faceted round peridot beads (G)
12	5mm by 7mm faceted flattened heart garnet beads (D)
30	5mm faceted rondel peridot beads (B)
36	4mm faceted rondel natural blue zircon beads (E)
42	15/0 gold-plated charlotte beads (C)
56	2mm hollow gold-filled round beads (A)
20	4mm vermeil daisy spacer beads (F)
1	14K gold box clasp
2	gold-filled crimp beads
2	gold-filled crimp bead covers
20"	of beading wire

TOPAZ AND "CORNFLAKES" NECKLACE

THIS NECKLACE IS A FINE EXAMPLE OF HOW MODERN ENHANCEMENTS HAVE INCREASED THE PALETTE OF THE JEWELRY DESIGNER. "LONDON BLUE" TOPAZ DID NOT EXIST UNTIL MODERN IRRADIATION TECHNIQUES WERE DEVELOPED.

1. First, arrange your topaz beads so that the largest bead is at the center and the smallest are at either end. The two beads on either side of the central bead should be of equal size and the whole arrangement should be balanced so that all opposing topaz beads match each other as closely as possible.

2. Start the necklace by threading on a crimp. Pass the beading wire through the ring of one half of the clasp and back through the crimp. Make sure that the beading wire is tight around the ring and squeeze the crimp shut.

3. Thread on 2 round gold beads so that they fit over the tail of the wire and cut away any excess. Then add 9 charlotte beads.

4. Using the arranged topaz beads, add a round gold bead, a Thai vermeil chip, a topaz bead, a vermeil chip, a gold round, 3 charlottes, a pearl, a charlotte, a pearl, a charlotte, another pearl, and 3 charlottes. Repeat this pattern 4 more times.

5. Now add 2 more charlottes, a round gold, a vermeil chip, and a topaz bead. Add another vermeil chip and then the central topaz bead. Add another vermeil chip, a topaz bead, a vermeil chip, a round gold, and 2 charlottes.

6. Now reverse the order in step 4 to make the other half of the necklace a mirror image of the first.

7. Add 9 charlottes, a gold round, and a crimp. Bring the beading wire through the ring of the other side of the clasp and back through the crimp and the round bead. Tighten the necklace so that there are no spaces between the beads, close the crimp, and snip off any remaining wire. Add the crimp covers.

TOOLS
Wire Cutters, Crimping Pliers

MATERIALS

13	oval-shaped "London Blue" topaz beads ranging in size from 8mm by 7mm to 11mm by 10mm
30	silver peacock, top-drilled cornflake pearls approximately 13mm in diameter
24	Thai vermeil chips approximately 4mm in diameter
84	size 13 gold-plated charlotte beads
22	2mm hollow gold-filled round beads
1	vermeil toggle clasp
2	gold-filled crimp beads
2	gold-filled crimp bead covers
20"	of beading wire

LABRADORITE ON CHAIN BRACELET

CHAIN CAN BE USED EITHER AS A MAJOR AESTHETIC ELEMENT OF A BRACELET OR SIMPLY AS THE STRUCTURAL FRAMEWORK. THESE FACETED LABRADORITE NUGGETS ARE SO DELIGHTFUL THAT I WANTED THEIR SHIMMERING IRIDESCENCE TO DOMINATE THE DESIGN, LETTING THE CHAIN SLIP INTO THE BACKGROUND. SILVER GOES SO WELL WITH LABRADORITE, HOWEVER, THAT I DID NOT WANT ITS INFLUENCE TO BE COMPLETELY LOST, AND I ADDED A FEW SILVER GRANULATED BEADS TO RESTORE BALANCE AND PROVIDE SOME CONTRASTING TEXTURE.

1. Begin by making the dangles. Add either a labradorite or a granulated silver bead and then a 1.5mm silver bead onto each headpin. If necessary, cut the headpin about ⅝" above the last bead and make a wire-wrapped loop.

2. Use the jump rings to attach the dangles and the clasp to the links of the chain. Start at the first link and attach the bar part of the toggle clasp using two jump rings to hold it securely. Reserve one labradorite and one silver dangle for the "tail" of the bracelet. Leaving 1 link empty, start adding the dangles to every link of the chain. The silver dangles should be placed at odd intervals between the labradorite. I have used 2 labradorite (L), then a silver (S), 5L, S, 5L, S, 5L, S, 6L, S, 5L. When you have added all the dangles (except the 2 reserved), use 2 jump rings to attach the next link to the other half of the clasp.

3. Now add a silver dangle to the last link of the chain and a labradorite dangle to the very last link. This creates the "tail" that hangs below the clasp.

TOOLS
Round-Nosed Pliers, Flat-Nosed Pliers, Wire Cutters

MATERIALS

	7½" of 7 by 5mm hammered silver flat cable chain
29	11mm by 10mm (approximately) faceted labradorite nuggets (L)
6	7mm Bali-style round granulated silver beads (S)
35	1.5mm faceted Thai silver round beads
39	5mm silver jump rings (at least 20 gauge in thickness)
35	1¼" silver headpins with ball tips
1	hammered silver toggle clasp

NOTE
When attaching dangles of this size to a chain bracelet, you need to use jump rings that are sufficiently sturdy. If the wire is too thin, there is a risk they will open with wear. Use a reasonably thick jump ring made from 20- or 18-gauge wire. If the bracelet is heavy, constant wear will place a lot of pressure on the jump rings that secure the clasp to the ends of the chain. For extra security, use two jump rings to attach each half of the clasp.

CLOCKWISE FROM TOP: Larimar Earrings; Serpentine, Carnelian, and Citrine Earrings;
Lapis Lazuli and Coral Earrings; Black Onyx and Gold Earrings; Precious Beryl Earrings

LARIMAR EARRINGS

THE EFFECT OF A BEAD CAP CAN SOMETIMES BE CREATED BY USING A DIFFERENT KIND OF BEAD. THESE HOLLOW GOLD BEADS SIT ON TOP OF THE LARIMAR WITHOUT EMBRACING IT, YET GIVE THE IMPRESSION OF A GOLDEN CROWN.

1. To each of the headpins add a daisy spacer, a larimar bead, an 18 karat gold disc, and a round gold bead. Begin a simple or a wrapped loop.

2. Slip the unfinished loop over the ring of the ear stud and close it by wire-wrapping.

TOOLS
Round-Nosed Pliers, Flat-Nosed Pliers

MATERIALS
- 2 9mm round larimar beads
- 2 4mm by 7mm puffed-disc 18 karat gold beads
- 2 2mm 18 karat gold daisy spacer beads
- 2 2mm hollow gold round beads
- 2 1" 18 karat gold headpins with ball tip
- 1 pair of 18 karat gold ear studs

SERPENTINE, CARNELIAN, AND CITRINE EARRINGS

HAVING A SLIGHTLY CREEPY NAME AND LOOKING SIMILAR TO JADE, IT IS HARDLY SURPRISING THAT SERPENTINE HAS SEVERAL OTHER, MORE ATTRACTIVE TRADE NAMES LIKE "SOO CHOW JADE" AND "NEW JADE." SOFTER AND LESS EXPENSIVE THAN REAL JADE, IT IS OFTEN FOUND IN CARVED SHAPES, SUCH AS THESE LEAVES.

1. To each 2" headpin add a 3mm gold bead, a serpentine leaf, a vermeil daisy spacer, a carnelian disc, another vermeil daisy spacer, 2 citrine beads, a daisy spacer, and a gold round bead.

2. Make a wire-wrapped loop. Open the loops of the earwires and attach the headpin loops.

TOOLS
Round-Nosed Pliers, Flat-Nosed Pliers, Wire Cutters

MATERIALS
- 2 20mm by 15mm serpentine carved leaf beads
- 2 10mm carnelian disc beads
- 4 5mm faceted rondel citrine beads
- 6 4mm vermeil daisy spacer beads
- 4 3mm seamless hollow gold-filled round beads
- 2 2" vermeil headpins with ball tip
- 1 pair of vermeil earwires

LAPIS LAZULI AND CORAL EARRINGS

BECAUSE OF ITS INCLUSIONS, LAPIS CAN HAVE A SOMEWHAT ORGANIC LOOK AND GOES WELL WITH CORAL.

1. First make the little dangles: add to each ¹/₂" headpin a 3mm coral bead and a 2mm gold bead. Make a simple loop.

2. To each 2" headpin add a 3mm gold bead, a 8mm gold bead, a lapis disc, a 5mm coral bead, 9 dangles, and a 3mm gold bead.

3. Cut the headpin ⁵/₈" above the last bead. Make the beginnings of a wire-wrapped loop. Attach this to the earwire and finish wrapping the tail of the headpin around the base of the loop.

TOOLS
Round-Nosed Pliers, Flat-Nosed Pliers, Wire Cutters

MATERIALS
18 3mm round red coral beads
2   5mm round red coral beads
2   13mm lapis lazuli flat disc beads
18 2mm seamless hollow gold-filled round beads
2   8mm seamless hollow gold-filled round beads
6   3mm seamless hollow gold-filled round beads
18 ¹/₂" vermeil headpins with ball tip
2   2" vermeil headpins with ball tip
1   pair of vermeil earwires

BLACK ONYX AND GOLD EARRINGS

LIKE A SIMPLE BLACK DRESS, ROUND, MATTE BLACK ONYX BEADS ARE THE MOST MODEST OF FASHIONS, BUT THEY CAN BE THE PERFECT COMPANION FOR THE RICHNESS OF GOLD. THESE ORNAMENTED VERMEIL BEAD CAPS PROVIDE PLENTY OF GLITTER, BUT THEY NEED THE RESTRAINT OF THE SOBER BLACK ONYX TO BE ELEGANT.

1. Start the earring by making the dangles. Add to each ¹/₂" headpin an onyx bead, a bead cap so that it fits over the onyx bead, and a round gold bead. Make a simple loop.

TOOLS
Round-Nosed Pliers, Flat-Nosed Pliers

MATERIALS
14 4mm round matte black onyx beads
14 6mm vermeil bead caps
2   1¹/₈" pieces of gold-filled "long and short" chain each with 3 long bars and 3 rings
14 2mm hollow gold-filled round beads
6   3.5mm gold-filled jump rings
2   3mm gold-filled jump rings
14 ¹/₂" vermeil headpins with ball tip
1   pair gold-filled earwires

2. Open the jump rings. Add 1 dangle to a 3mm jump ring and attach it to the ring at one end of the chain. Close the jump ring. Use a 3.5mm jump ring to add 2 dangles to the next ring of the chain. Repeat this to add another 2 dangles to the next ring of the chain.

3. Attach the end of the chain to the earwire (either by opening the loop of the earwire or slipping it over the hook, depending on the style). Add two dangles to a jump ring and attach it to the loop of the earwire. Close the jump ring.

PRECIOUS BERYL EARRINGS

A BEAUTIFUL GEMSTONE BEAD REQUIRES LITTLE TO BECOME A STRIKING EARRING. PRECIOUS BERYL IS ALSO KNOWN AS MORGANITE AND PINK AQUAMARINE, BUT THE QUALITY OF THESE BEADS CALLS FOR THE MORE EXPENSIVE-SOUNDING TITLE. GEMS OF THIS QUALITY ARE BEST PAIRED WITH REAL GOLD.

TOOLS
Round-Nosed Pliers, Flat-Nosed Pliers, Wire Cutters

1. To each of the 1½" headpins, add a daisy spacer bead, a precious beryl bead, and another daisy spacer. Cut the headpin about a ¼" above the last bead and make a simple loop.

2. Open the headpin loops to attach them to the loops of the ear studs.

MATERIALS
2   18mm by 12mm lozenge-shaped precious beryl (pink aquamarine) beads

4   2mm 18 karat gold daisy spacer beads

2   1½" 18 karat gold headpins with ball tip

1   pair of decorated 18 karat gold ear studs

CLOCKWISE FROM TOP LEFT: Pink Sapphire Earrings, Tanzanite and Ruby Earrings,
Black Spinel and Garnet Earrings, Carnelian and Turquoise Earrings

PINK SAPPHIRE EARRINGS

YOU CAN OFTEN BUY DROPS, SUCH AS THESE SAPPHIRES,
WITH WIRE LOOPS SO THAT THEY ARE READY TO USE AS LITTLE
PENDANTS. UNLESS YOU ARE SKILLED AT WIRE-WRAPPING,
BUYING THEM THIS WAY PRODUCES A BETTER FINISHED LOOK
AND YOU CAN SKIP STEP 1.

1. If you are using beads without loops, start by making the wire loops for all the drops. Cut a piece of wire 1" long. Thread it through the hole of the bead and bend it back on itself so that about $3/16$" is above the bead, lying parallel to the tail of the wire.

2. Use the round-nosed pliers to make a loop on the tail so that the bottom of the loop touches the top of the other end of the wire. The wire should now look like a figure eight. Wrap the tail around the middle of the figure eight, enclosing the other end of the wire. Cut away any excess wire. Measure the excess wire and subtract that length from 1". Use this length to cut all the other pieces of wire so that they are exactly to size.

3. Open the jump rings and use them to attach the loops of the drops to each of the loops of the ear hoops.

TOOLS
Flat-Nosed Pliers, Round-Nosed Pliers, Wire Cutters

MATERIALS
14 6mm by 4mm faceted top-drilled teardrop pink sapphire beads with wire loops

14 2.5mm gold-filled jump rings

1 pair of gold-filled ear hoops with 7 loops

12" of 30 gauge gold-filled wire (if the beads did not come with loops)

TANZANITE AND RUBY EARRINGS

IT IS NOW QUITE COMMON TO FIND GEMSTONE DROPS SOLD
WITH WIRE LOOPS ALREADY ATTACHED, MAKING THEM VERY
EASY TO USE. AS LONG AS THE WIRE IS OF GOOD QUALITY, THIS IS
A CONVENIENT WAY TO SAVE SOME TIME IN MAKING EARRINGS.

1. Start by creating the chain of tanzanite rondels. Cut the wire into
   1" pieces. At the end of 1 piece of wire, make a very small
   wire-wrapped loop, only making 1 turn around (this should use
   about $^3/_8$" of the wire). Add a tanzanite rondel and make the
   beginnings of another wire-wrapped loop. Add a 3.5mm gold
   ring to the loop and finish it off with 1 turn around the base of
   the loop, making sure it is tight against the tanzanite bead.

2. At the end of another piece of wire, make the beginnings of a
   loop. Slip it over the ring that is attached to the link you have
   just made and finish it with 1 turn around. Add a tanzanite bead,
   start another loop, add another ring, and finish it off. Repeat this
   step another 4 times. You now have a chain of tanzanite beads
   with a ring at either end and 5 rings between the beads.

3. Add a tanzanite bead to a headpin and make the beginnings of a
   wire-wrapped loop. Add this to the first of the rings between the
   beads on the chain you have just made. Close the loop, wrapping
   the wire several times around the base. Add a tanzanite bead to
   another headpin and attach it to the same ring in the same
   manner. Repeat this process until there are 2 of these dangles on
   each of the rings between the tanzanite beads of the chain.

4. Use a 4mm jump ring to attach 3 of the ruby beads to the ring at
   one end of the chain.

5. Use a 3mm jump ring to attach the ring at the other end of the
   chain to the loop of the ear stud. Make the other earring in the
   same manner.

TOOLS
Round-Nosed Pliers, Flat-Nosed Pliers, Wire
Cutters

MATERIALS

32	2mm by 3mm tanzanite faceted rondel beads
6	5mm by 7mm ruby faceted top-drilled drops (briolettes) with gold wire loops (If you cannot find the briolettes with wire loops, make wire-wrapped loops using 30 gauge gold-filled wire.)
14	3.5mm gold-filled rings
2	3mm gold-filled jump rings
2	4mm gold-filled jump rings
20	$^1/_2$" vermeil headpins with ball tip
12"	of 30 gauge gold-filled wire
1	pair of 18 karat gold ear studs

NOTE
You need very fine-tipped round-nosed pliers
to make the wire-wrapped loops.

BLACK SPINEL AND GARNET EARRINGS

HERE IS AN INTERESTING WAY TO USE CHAIN TO CREATE
EARRINGS. BY SELECTING THE CENTRAL LINK IN A THREE-
LINK PIECE OF CHAIN, IT ALLOWS ONE OF THE LINKS TO
FALL BACK ON TOP OF THE OTHER, MAKING A NICE FRAME
FOR THE TINY GARNET.

1. Start by using a jump ring to attach the middle link of a piece of
   chain to the loop of the earwire. When you hold up the earwire,
   one of the circular links should now fall down so that it is
   hanging over half the oblong link.

2. Add a garnet bead to a $^1/_2$" headpin and attach it to the bottom of
   the pendulant circular ring by making a simple loop.

3. Add to a $^3/_4$" headpin a black spinel cone and a 2mm round gold
   bead. Make a simple loop and attach it to the bottom of the
   oblong link of the chain.

TOOLS
Round-Nosed Pliers, Flat-Nosed Pliers

MATERIALS

- 2 sections of chain, each with 2 circular
  links and 1 oblong link (The circular links
  are 10mm in diameter and the oblong is
  20mm in length.)
- 2 8mm faceted cone-shaped black spinel
  drops
- 2 1.5mm faceted round garnet beads
- 2 2mm hollow gold-filled round beads
- 2 $^1/_2$" gold-filled headpins with ball tip
- 2 $^3/_4$" gold-filled headpins with ball tip
- 2 4mm gold-filled jump rings
- 1 pair of gold-filled earwires

CARNELIAN AND TURQUOISE EARRINGS

(Page 72, below left)

THE EASY WAY TO MAKE THESE EARRINGS IS TO BUY THE TURQUOISE CHAIN ALREADY PREPARED. BUT IF YOU ARE FEELING CONFIDENT IN YOUR ABILITY TO MAKE TINY WIRE-WRAPPED LOOPS AND HAVE TIME TO SPARE, YOU CAN MAKE THEM YOURSELF WITH LOOSE TURQUOISE BEADS AND 28 GAUGE GOLD-FILLED WIRE.

1. To each of the 1½" eyepins, add a gold round bead, a vermeil disc, a carnelian bicone, a vermeil disc, and another gold round bead. Cut the eyepin about a ¼" above the last bead and make a simple loop.

2. Attach the loop you have just made to one end of the turquoise chain. Use a 3mm jump ring to attach the other end of the chain to the earwire loop.

3. Use a 4mm jump ring to attach a vermeil flat disc to the loop of the eyepin.

TOOLS

Round-Nosed Pliers, Flat-Nosed Pliers, Wire Cutters

MATERIALS

2   10mm faceted carnelian bicone beads

2   34mm lengths (1³/₈") of chain with 3mm turquoise round beads

2   11mm vermeil flat discs with stamped or cast design

4   3mm vermeil discs (torus)

4   2.5mm hollow gold-filled round beads

4   3mm gold-filled jump rings

2   4mm gold-filled jump rings

2   1½" vermeil eyepins

1   pair of vermeil earwires

TIP:

You can make your own eyepins from 24 gauge gold-filled wire. Just cut the wire to the length you need, plus ¼". Then make a simple loop at the end of the wire.

CLOCKWISE FROM TOP LEFT: Watermelon Tourmaline Earrings,
London Blue Topaz Earrings, Mother-of-Pearl and Lapis Earrings

WATERMELON TOURMALINE EARRINGS

UTTERLY SIMPLE AND TOTALLY ELEGANT, THESE EARRINGS SHOW OFF SLICES OF TRANSLUCENT TOURMALINE TO STUNNING EFFECT. IT IS ALMOST IRRESISTIBLE TO MAKE YOUR OWN JEWELRY WHEN A FEW MINUTES' EFFORT CAN PRODUCE SOMETHING AS BEAUTIFUL AS THIS.

1. To a headpin, add a tourmaline slice and an amethyst bead. Make a simple loop.

2. Attach the loop to the earwire by opening and closing it.

TOOLS
Round-Nosed Pliers, Flat-Nosed Pliers, Wire Cutters

MATERIALS
- 2   10mm side-drilled slices of watermelon tourmaline
- 2   2mm amethyst round beads
- 2 $^3/_4$" silver headpins with ball tip
- 1   pair of silver stringer earwires

LONDON BLUE TOPAZ EARRINGS

BEAD CAPS PROVIDE A SIMPLE AND INEXPENSIVE WAY OF DRESSING UP A SINGLE GEMSTONE BEAD. USED IN EARRINGS, THEY CAN CREATE LITTLE ACORNLIKE JEWELS. THE HANDCRAFTED NATURE OF THESE CAPS GIVES THEM A SLIGHTLY IRREGULAR APPEARANCE, AS IF THEY WERE TRULY FROM NATURE. USING A BEAD CAP CAN ALSO BE A GREAT WAY OF COVERING A BLEMISH ON AN OTHERWISE BEAUTIFUL STONE.

1. To each of the $1^1/_2$" headpins, add a topaz, a bead cap so that it fits over the topaz, and a round silver bead. Cut the headpin about $^5/_8$" above the last bead and make a wire-wrapped loop.

2. Open the jump rings and use them to attach the headpin loops to the loops of the earwires.

TOOLS
Round-Nosed Pliers, Flat-Nosed Pliers, Wire Cutters

MATERIALS
- 2   10mm by 8mm lozenge-shaped London blue topaz beads
- 2   8mm by 11mm handcrafted Thai silver bead caps
- 2   3mm seamless hollow silver round beads
- 2 $1^1/_2$" silver headpins with ball tip
- 2   4mm silver jump rings
- 1   pair of silver earwires

MOTHER-OF-PEARL AND LAPIS EARRINGS

MOTHER-OF-PEARL IS THE NACREOUS PART OF A MOLLUSK SHELL. BECAUSE IT IS COMPOSED OF THE SAME MATERIAL AS THE PEARL, IT HAS SIMILAR CHARACTERISTICS AND CAN SOMETIMES DISPLAY AN EVEN FINER IRIDESCENCE. THESE LOVELY BEADS ARE COMPOSED OF SMALL TILES OF LAPIS LAZULI AND MOTHER-OF-PEARL BONDED TOGETHER IN A CHECKERBOARD PATTERN.

1. To a headpin, add a checkerboard bead and a silver round bead. Cut the headpin about $5/16$" above the round bead and make a simple loop.

2. Use a 5mm jump ring to attach this to the rim of the silver hoop. Attach a 4mm jump ring to an earwire.

3. Use another 5mm jump ring to attach the 4mm jump ring to the rim of the silver hoop that is opposite to the checkerboard bead. (Note: You must use two jump rings to attach the earwire to make the earring hang properly.)

TOOLS
Flat-Nosed Pliers, Round-Nosed Pliers, Wire Cutters

MATERIALS
- 2 12mm mother-of-pearl and lapis lazuli "checkerboard" flat square beads, diagonally drilled
- 2 22mm silver decorated hoops with 3mm flat rims
- 2 2mm hollow silver round beads
- 4 5mm silver jump rings
- 2 4mm silver jump rings
- 2 $1^1/2$" silver headpins with ball tip
- 1 pair of silver stringer earwires

SMOOTH AQUAMARINE NECKLACE

AQUAMARINE USED TO BE PRIZED FOR ITS "SEA-GREEN" COLOR, BUT AS TASTES HAVE TURNED TO TROPICAL BLUE WATER, SO HAS THAT COLOR BECOME MORE POPULAR. THE LOVELY PINK FORM OF THE STONE IS ALSO PROPERLY CALLED "MORGANITE" (NAMED AFTER THE AMERICAN BANKER AND COLLECTOR OF GEMSTONE, J.P. MORGAN), BUT IT SOUNDS A LOT MORE ROMANTIC TO CALL IT "PINK AQUAMARINE." ALL OF THEM ARE PRECIOUS BERYL. MOST AQUAMARINE IS HEAT-TREATED TO TRY TO ACHIEVE THE CURRENT IDEAL PALE BLUE COLOR, BUT THESE LOVELY STONES ARE NATURAL. THE CLOUDY NATURE COULD BE SEEN AS A LACK OF CLARITY, BUT FOR ME, IT GIVES THE STONE A DELIGHTFUL CHARACTER THAT I FIND MORE INTERESTING THAN THE CLEAR VARIETY. THE CLOUDINESS HAS THE OTHER BENEFIT OF MAKING SUCH LARGE STONES MORE AFFORDABLE BECAUSE IF CLEAR AQUAMARINE GEMS WERE THIS HUGE, THEY WOULD BE HUGELY EXPENSIVE.

1. Unless the strand you have bought is strung exactly the way you want it, start by laying out the stones in a color and size arrangement that pleases you. Start the necklace by threading on a crimp. Pass the beading wire through the ring of one half of the clasp and back through the crimp. Make sure that the beading wire is tight around the ring and squeeze the crimp shut.

2. Thread on a gold round bead so that it fits over the tail of the wire and cut away any excess. Then add 4 more gold beads. Add the gemstone beads in the order in which they are laid out, putting 3 gold beads between each gemstone. Try the necklace around your neck to make sure that the length and color arrangement please you.

3. Add another 5 gold beads and a crimp. Bring the beading wire through the ring of the other side of the clasp and back through the crimp and the round bead. Now tighten the necklace so that there are no spaces between the beads, close the crimp and snip off any remaining beading wire. Add the crimp covers.

TOOLS
Wire Cutters, Crimping Pliers

MATERIALS (FOR A 22" NECKLACE)

1	18" strand of graduated aquamarine in smooth, tumbled shapes ranging from 13mm to 33mm in size
70	2mm 18 karat gold round beads
1	18 karat box clasp
2	gold-filled crimp beads
2	gold-filled crimp bead covers
26"	of beading wire

DIAMONDS IN THE ROUGH

UNTIL A FEW YEARS AGO, DIAMONDS WERE THE EXCLUSIVE PROVINCE OF PROFESSIONAL JEWELERS WHO NEEDED TO SET THEM IN PRECIOUS METAL BEFORE THEY COULD BE USED. DIAMONDS ARE 140 TIMES HARDER THAN THE NEXT HARDEST GEMSTONE AND DRILLING THEM WAS NOT AN OPTION. THE INVENTION OF THE LASER DRILL, HOWEVER, HAS AT LAST MADE POSSIBLE THE CREATION OF DIAMOND BEADS. UNFORTUNATELY, TECHNOLOGY HAS NOT MADE THESE DESIRABLE GEMS ANY LESS EXPENSIVE AND THE VISION OF A ROPE OF CUT AND POLISHED DIAMONDS IS STILL ONLY A REALITY FOR THE VERY RICH AND A DREAM FOR THE REST OF US. BUT SMALL, ROUGH DIAMONDS CAN BE BOUGHT FOR HUNDREDS OF DOLLARS A STRAND RATHER THAN HUNDREDS OF THOUSANDS. ALTHOUGH THEY EXPRESS ONLY THE OCCASIONAL FLASH OF DIAMOND SPARKLE, ROUGH DIAMONDS HAVE A DISTINCTIVE CHARACTER, SUBTLE BUT STILL EMPHATIC. LIKE ALL DIAMONDS, THESE HAVE INVESTMENT VALUE, SO YOU HAVE THE PLEASURE OF WEARING YOUR WEALTH AROUND YOUR NECK.

1. Start the necklace by threading on a crimp. Pass the beading wire through the ring of one half of the clasp and back through the crimp. Make sure that the beading wire is tight around the ring and squeeze the crimp shut.

2. Add a gold bead and then a few diamond beads. The gold beads are going to be scattered among the diamond beads in a random fashion. So you don't use up the gold beads too quickly, divide them into 3 equal portions and use 1 portion for each of the diamond strands. For an idea of random spacing, refer to the picture of the necklace. Save 1 gold bead as the last bead before the crimp. Add all the diamond beads, separating them at random points with 1 or 2 gold beads.

3. Add the final gold bead and a crimp. Bring the beading wire through the ring of the other side of the clasp and back through the crimp. Tighten the necklace so that there are no spaces between the beads, close the crimp, and snip off any remaining beading wire.

TOOLS
Crimping Pliers, Wire Cutters

MATERIALS (FOR A 49" ROPE)

3 14" strands of 3mm rough diamond beads

1 7" strand of 2mm 18 karat gold faceted round beads

1 18 karat gold hook-and-eye clasp

1 4mm 18 karat gold ring

54" of size 0.13 beading wire

GREEN KYANITE SHARDS NECKLACE

THE NAME *KYANITE* COMES FROM THE GREEK WORD FOR "BLUE," BUT AS YOU CAN SEE IN THIS NECKLACE, THE STONE IS SOMETIMES FOUND IN PLEASANT SHADES OF GREEN. I HAVE USED A GRADUATED STRAND OF SHARDS THAT, ROUGHLY CUT AND POLISHED, GIVES AN IMPRESSION OF THE NATURAL CRYSTAL. THIS KYANITE IS NEITHER HIGH QUALITY NOR VERY EXPENSIVE, BUT THE UNUSUAL COLOR AND SHAPE OF THE SHARDS, AS WELL AS THEIR BROAD SURFACE AREA, HELP MAKE THIS A PARTICULARLY INTERESTING GEMSTONE DISPLAY.

1. Start the necklace by threading on a crimp. Pass the beading wire through the ring of one half of the clasp and back through the crimp. Make sure that the beading wire is tight around the ring and squeeze the crimp shut.

2. Thread on a silver round bead so that it fits over the tail of the wire and cut away any excess. Add a black onyx bead and a faceted silver bead. Repeat this 3 times and add an additional black onyx bead.

3. Take the first kyanite bead off the temporary strand and add it to the wire followed by a black onyx bead. Repeat this with the rest of the kyanite beads, being sure to thread them on so that the graduation remains the same as it was on the temporary strand and that there is a black onyx bead after each kyanite shard.

4. Add a faceted silver bead and a black onyx bead. Repeat 3 times and then add the remaining silver round bead and a crimp. Bring the beading wire through the ring of the other side of the clasp and back through the crimp and the round bead. Tighten the necklace so that there are no spaces between the beads, close the crimp, and snip off any remaining beading wire. Add the crimp covers.

TOOLS
Wire Cutters, Crimping Pliers

MATERIALS
- 1 14" graduated strand of green kyanite with shards from 10mm to 35mm long
- 60 2mm black onyx round beads (You might need a few more or less depending on the number of kyanite shards.)
- 2 2.5mm hollow silver round beads
- 8 2mm faceted silver spacer beads
- 1 silver toggle clasp
- 2 silver crimp beads
- 2 silver crimp bead covers
- 20" of beading wire

THAI SAPPHIRES NECKLACE

THAILAND IS WELL-KNOWN FOR ITS SOPHISTICATED TECHNIQUE OF CHANGING THE COLOR OF SAPPHIRES THROUGH HEAT TREATMENT. BECAUSE THE COLOR CHANGE IS PERMANENT AND BECAUSE MANY OF THE STONES ARE OF STUNNING QUALITY, THAI SAPPHIRES HAVE BECOME BOTH FAMOUS AND DESIRABLE. THE COLORS THAT CAN BE ACHIEVED THROUGH HEAT-TREATING ARE SO VARIED AND DELICIOUS THAT A SINGLE STRAND OF VERY SMALL BRIOLETTES CAN CREATE A GLITTERING RAINBOW AROUND THE NECK.

1. Start the necklace by threading on a crimp. Pass the beading wire through the ring of one half of the clasp and back through the crimp. Make sure that the beading wire is tight around the ring and squeeze the crimp shut.

2. Thread on 9 gold spacer beads so that as many as possible fit over the tail of the wire. If there is any excess tail, cut it away.

3. Now add the sapphires in the order you have arranged them, separating each bead with a gold spacer bead.

4. Add 9 gold spacer beads and a crimp. Bring the beading wire through the ring of the other side of the clasp and back through the crimp and the gold beads (as many of them as the wire passes through easily). Now tighten the necklace so that there are no spaces between the beads. Important: Before closing the crimp, make sure that each of the briolettes is facing the opposite direction to its neighbor. Tighten again, close the crimp, and snip off any remaining beading wire.

WHEN HEART-SHAPED BRIOLETTES ARE STRUNG CLOSELY TOGETHER WITH ONLY A TINY SEPARATION, THEY NATURALLY ASSUME A POSITION WHERE EACH IS POINTING IN THE OPPOSITE DIRECTION TO ITS NEIGHBOR. THIS EFFECTIVELY DOUBLES THE WIDTH OF THE BAND, INCREASING THE PERCEIVED SIZE OF THE GEMSTONES. BECAUSE OF THE GREAT VARIETY OF COLORS, THE TEMPORARY STRAND YOU PURCHASE MAY BE ARRANGED IN A PLEASING ORDER; OTHERWISE, LAY OUT YOUR SAPPHIRES FIRST SO THAT THE COLORS ARE BALANCED. USE THE PICTURE OF THE NECKLACE FOR AN IDEA OF HOW A HARMONIOUS ARRANGEMENT CAN BE ACHIEVED.

TOOLS
Wire Cutters, Crimping Pliers

MATERIALS (FOR A 15" CHOKER)

- 1   14" strand of multicolored Thai sapphire heart-shaped briolettes 5mm by 5mm in size

- 110   3mm 18 karat gold daisy spacer beads (You might need more or less depending on the number of sapphires.)

- 1   18 karat gold toggle clasp

- 2   gold-filled mini-crimp beads (1mm by 1mm)

- 20"   of 0.13 beading wire (gold color is preferable)

WHEN BLACK IS BRILLIANT

THERE ARE SEVERAL BLACK GEMSTONES, INCLUDING HEMATITE, BLACK ONYX, OBSIDIAN, AND JET, THE LAST GIVING ITS NAME TO THAT ULTIMATE DARKNESS, "JET BLACK." ALTHOUGH THEIR ABSENCE OF COLOR IS SIMILAR, THEY ARE DIFFERENTIATED BY THEIR LUSTER, AND IT IS BLACK SPINEL THAT, WITH THE EXCEPTION OF BLACK DIAMOND, OWNS THE TOP POSITION IN THE SPARKLE CATEGORY. SPINEL IS A HARD STONE WITH VERY GOOD REFLECTIVITY; THE RED VARIETY WAS PREVIOUSLY THOUGHT TO BE A TYPE OF RUBY AND EQUALLY PRIZED. IN THE BLACK VERSION OF THE STONE, QUALITY DEPENDS ON EXCELLENT CUTTING TO MAXIMIZE ITS WONDERFUL REFLECTIVE PROPERTIES.

1. Start the necklace by threading on a crimp. Pass the beading wire through the ring of one half of the clasp and back through the crimp. Make sure that the beading wire is tight around the ring and squeeze the crimp shut. Cut off any tail of the wire as close to the crimp bead as possible.

2. Thread on 7 silver beads and a spinel briolette. Repeat this pattern 25 times.

3. Add a further 7 silver beads and a crimp. Bring the beading wire through the ring of the other side of the clasp and back through the crimp. Tighten the necklace so that there are no spaces between the beads, close the crimp, and snip off any remaining beading wire. Add the crimp covers.

TOOLS
Wire Cutters, Crimping Pliers

MATERIALS
26 10mm by 10mm flattened heart-shaped black spinel briolettes

189 (about a 14" strand) 1mm by 1mm faceted Thai silver beads

1 silver "stardust" toggle clasp

2 silver crimp beads

2 silver crimp bead covers

20" of beading wire

WATERMELON SLICES NECKLACE

ALTHOUGH MANY GEMSTONES ARE VALUED FOR THEIR
CONSISTENCY AND REGULARITY, SOME ARE TREASURED FOR THE
VERY OPPOSITE. "WATERMELON" TOURMALINE IS ONE OF THE
MOST BEAUTIFUL OF THE LATTER. TOURMALINE CAN COME IN
MANY DIFFERENT COLORS, AND OCCASIONALLY CRYSTALS ARE
FOUND WITH A CORE OF ONE COLOR AND AN OUTER LAYER OF
ANOTHER. WHEN THESE CRYSTALS ARE SLICED, THE BEAUTIFUL
PATTERN IS DISPLAYED TO ITS GREATEST ADVANTAGE. OFTEN,
THE SLICES HAVE A PINK INTERIOR AND GREEN "SKIN" THAT IS
REMINISCENT OF A SLICED WATERMELON. INCREASINGLY
DIFFICULT TO FIND, GOOD WATERMELON TOURMALINE IS
SOMETHING TO ACQUIRE WHEN YOU SEE IT. IN SMALL SIZES,
THE PURPLE TONES OF AMETHYST BECOME MORE SUBDUED,
MAKING THEM GOOD SPACERS TO SHOW OFF THE TOURMALINE.

1. Thread a crimp on the beading wire. Pass the wire through the ring of one half of the clasp and back through the crimp. Make sure that the beading wire is tight around the ring and squeeze the crimp shut. Thread on a 3mm silver bead so that it fits over the tail of the wire and cut off any excess wire.

2. Thread on three 2mm amethyst beads and a tourmaline slice.

3. Add five 2mm amethyst beads and a tourmaline slice. Repeat this pattern 8 times. Add three 2mm amethyst beads, a tourmaline bead, and 3 more amethyst beads. Reverse and repeat the 5 amethyst bead and 1 tourmaline pattern from this step 10 times, to mirror the first half of the necklace.

4. Now add three 2mm amethyst beads and the other 3mm silver bead and a crimp. Bring the beading wire through the ring of the other side of the clasp and back through the crimp and the first round silver bead. Tighten the necklace so that all the beads are snugly together, close the crimp, and snip off any remaining beading wire. Add the crimp covers.

5. Add the final tourmaline slice to the headpin and make a wire-wrapped loop. Use the jump ring to attach this pendant to the last ring of the clasp.

TOOLS
Wire Cutters, Crimping Pliers

MATERIALS (FOR A 20" NECKLACE)
- 22 10mm to 12mm side-drilled slices of watermelon tourmaline
- 102 2mm amethyst round beads
- 2 3mm hollow seamless silver round beads
- 1 5mm silver jump ring
- 1 ³/₄" silver headpin
- 1 silver toggle extension clasp
- 2 silver crimp beads
- 2 silver crimp bead covers
- 20" of beading wire

NOTE
The use of an extension clasp allows you to adjust the necklace length, by up to an inch, when you wear it.

THREE-STRAND TOURMALINE NECKLACE

A SINGLE STRAND OF TINY GEMSTONES CAN BE STRETCHED OUT TO PROVIDE ENOUGH MATERIAL FOR AN EFFECTIVE THREE-STRAND NECKLACE. FOR THIS DESIGN I USED A VARIETY OF GLASS CHARLOTTE BEADS TO EXTEND THE GEMS. BECAUSE CHARLOTTES HAVE ONE FLAT FACET, THEY ADD AN OCCASIONAL SPARKLE TO THE MANY LITTLE GEMSTONES.

1. To make the doubled strand, start with 36" of beading wire. Fold it in half. Add a 4mm ring to the wire so that it sits in the middle where you have folded it. Pass both the ends of the wire through a crimp and make it snug against the ring. Once you are sure the ring is positioned in the middle of the wire, close the crimp so that the wire is tight around the ring. You should now have 2 wires of equal length joined at the end by the crimped ring.

2. Add your tourmaline and charlottes to 1 of the doubled strands. The pattern is random, so use your judgment or refer to the photograph for guidance. When you have a completed a strand 16" long, put tape around the end of the beading wire to keep the beads from falling off.

3. Then fill the other side of the doubled wire with gems and charlottes. As you do this, compare the colors of the tourmaline to the first strand so you avoid putting the same colors exactly opposite each other. This time make the strand 16¼" long. Holding the wire ends so that the beads can't fall off, remove the tape and insert both ends into a crimp bead. Bring the wire through another 6mm ring and back through the crimp. Before you squeeze the crimp shut, it is important that you adjust the wires so that the beads are all snug, with no gaps between them. Remember, the first wire is going to be a little shorter than the second, so tighten them accordingly.

4. For the single strand, cut a piece of beading wire 20" long. Use a crimp to attach one end to a jump ring and fill it with gems and charlottes to a length of 16½". Add a crimp, make sure all the beads are snug and attach it to the final jump ring.

5. Cut the gold-filled wire into two halves. Pass the end of one piece through one ring of the single strand and one ring of the doubled strand and make a wire-wrapped loop to secure them. Now add a cone to the wire, so that it sits down on the rings, covering the ends of both strands. Tug the end of the wire to make sure the fit is snug and add a round gold bead. Make the beginning of a wire-wrapped loop but, before closing it, slip on one of the clasp halves and complete the wrapping to close the loop. Repeat this step to attach the other side of the necklace to the clasp.

TOOLS
Wire Cutters, Crimping Pliers, Round-Nosed Pliers, Flat-Nosed Pliers, Transparent Adhesive Tape

MATERIALS

1	16" strand of multicolor 3mm tourmaline faceted rondels
3	12" strands of size 13/0 charlotte beads, 1 gold-plated, 1 bronze-plated, and 1 gunmetal
2	3mm hollow seamless gold-filled round beads
1	9mm vermeil toggle clasp
2	11mm vermeil cones
4	4mm gold-filled jump rings
2"	of 20 gauge gold-filled wire
6	gold-filled crimp beads
56"	of beading wire

NOTE
One of the strands is single and one double. The end of each strand is attached to one of the 4mm rings. One pair of rings holds the single strand and the other pair holds the doubled strand. The wire is used to hold the rings and is passed through the cones to secure everything to the clasp.

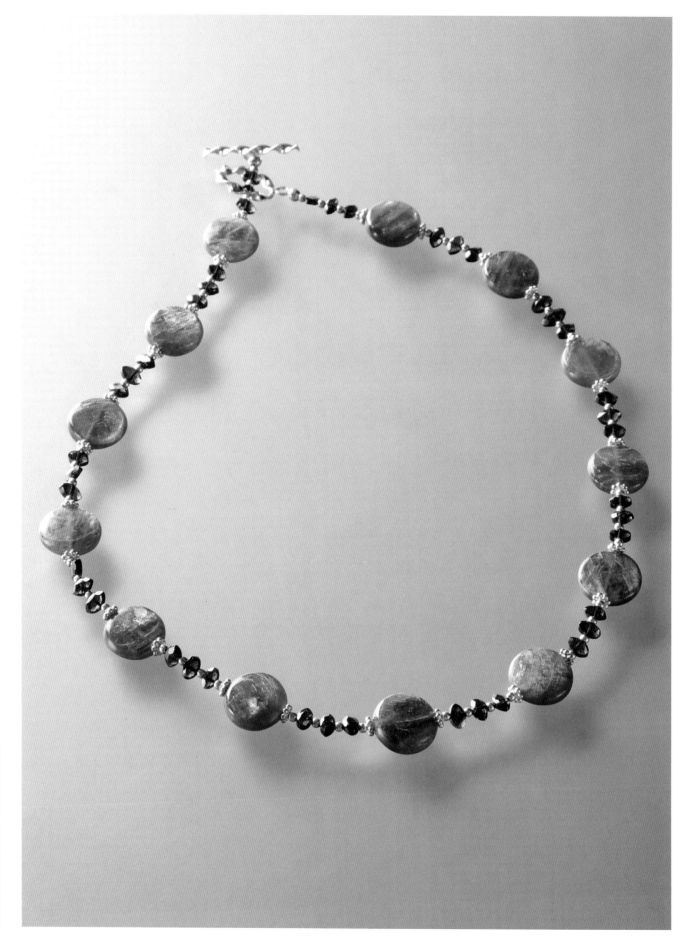

KYANITE WITH GARNETS NECKLACE

KYANITE HAS LOTS OF CHARACTER, WHICH IS BEAUTIFULLY
DISPLAYED IN THESE DISCS. THE BROAD SURFACE SHOWS THE
VARIATION AND INTERNAL REFLECTIVITY TO GREAT ADVANTAGE,
AND THE THINNESS OF THE DISC MAKES THE PIECES FAR LESS
COSTLY THAN THE SAME-SIZED ROUND BEADS. RED AND BLUE
ARE A CLASSIC COMBINATION, AND THE SLIGHTLY VIOLET HUE OF
THE GARNETS HELPS THEM BLEND PARTICULARLY WELL WITH
THE COLOR OF THE KYANITE. USING THREE SMALL GARNETS FOR
EACH LARGE DISC BALANCES THE TWO STONES IN PROPER
HARMONY.

1. Start the necklace by threading on a crimp. Pass the beading
    wire through the ring of one half of the clasp and back through
    the crimp. Make sure that the beading wire is tight around the
    ring and squeeze the crimp shut.

2. Thread on a silver round bead, a garnet bead, another silver
    round, another garnet, another silver round, a garnet, and a
    silver round. Then add a daisy, a kyanite disc, and another daisy.

3. Repeat this pattern 12 times.

4. Add a silver round, garnet, silver round, garnet, silver round,
    garnet, silver round, and a crimp. Bring the beading wire
    through the ring of the other side of the clasp and back through
    the crimp and a round bead. Tighten the necklace so there are
    no spaces between the beads, close the crimp, and snip off any
    remaining beading wire. Add the crimp covers.

TOOLS
Wire Cutters, Crimping Pliers

MATERIALS

13	12mm to 13mm flat disc kyanite beads
42	3mm by 6mm side-drilled marquise garnet beads
56	2mm hollow silver round beads
26	4mm silver daisy spacer beads
1	silver toggle clasp
2	silver crimp beads
2	silver crimp bead covers
22"	of beading wire

AMETHYST AND DICHROIC GLASS NECKLACE

THE COLOR OF AMETHYST CAN BE DIFFICULT TO WORK WITH. ITS INTENSE PURPLE CAN CLASH WITH OTHER BEADS AND SOMETIMES OVERWHELMS THE WEARER, RATHER THAN FLATTERING HER. IN THIS DESIGN, HOWEVER, AMETHYST COMPLEMENTS THE DICHROIC GLASS PENDANTS, AND THE EQUAL AMOUNT OF SILVER DILUTES AND BALANCES THE INTENSITY OF THE PURPLE.

1. Start by making the pendants. Add a silver daisy, a 6mm lapis bead, another daisy, a 4mm amethyst bead, and a 2mm silver round. Make a simple loop or a wire-wrapped loop. Repeat this pattern for 2 more pendants, then make the final 2 pendants, substituting 6mm amethyst beads for the 6mm lapis, and 4mm lapis beads for the 4mm amethyst.

2. Use the jump rings to attach the pendants to the pendant hanger as shown.

3. Thread a crimp on the beading wire. Pass the wire through the ring of one half of the clasp and back through the crimp. Make sure that the beading wire is tight around the ring and squeeze the crimp shut. Thread on a 3mm silver bead so that it fits over the tail of the wire and cut off any excess.

4. Thread on a 6mm amethyst bead and 3 silver daisy spacer beads. Repeat this pattern 15 times. Then add a 6mm lapis bead, 3 more daisy spacers, and a 6mm amethyst bead. Next, add 1 daisy and a 3mm silver bead.

5. Now add the pendant hanger followed by a 3mm silver bead, a daisy spacer, a 6mm amethyst bead, 3 daisy spacers, and a 6mm lapis bead.

6. Add 3 daisy spacers and a 6mm amethyst bead. Repeat this pattern 15 times. Add a 3mm silver round and the crimp. Bring the beading wire through the ring of the other side of the clasp and back through the crimp and the round bead. Close the crimp, and snip off any remaining wire. Add the crimp covers.

TOOLS
Wire Cutters, Crimping Pliers

MATERIALS
36 6mm amethyst round beads
3 4mm amethyst round beads
5 6mm lapis lazuli round beads
2 4mm lapis lazuli round beads
5 dichroic glass pendants with 1" silver wire stems
114 5mm silver daisy spacer beads
4 3mm hollow silver round beads
5 2mm hollow silver round beads
5 5mm silver jump rings
1 40mm silver curved pendant hanger with 5 loops
1 silver toggle clasp
2 silver crimp beads
2 silver crimp bead covers
22" of beading wire

MULTISTONE NECKLACE

FACETED RONDELS ARE OFTEN SOLD AS A STRAND OF MIXED GEMSTONES, KNOWN AS A "MULTISTONE" STRAND. CONTAINING GEMS SUCH AS PERIDOT, GARNET, AMETHYST, IOLITE, TOPAZ, AND TOURMALINE, THESE STRANDS OFFER AN EASY WAY TO CREATE A MULTICOLORED NECKLACE OR BRACELET.

1. Start the necklace by making the "dangles." Pick out 50 of the multistone beads so that you have a roughly equal number of each color. Add one vermeil daisy bead, one multistone bead, a 3mm gold round bead, and a 1/2" headpin. Make a simple loop. Repeat this until you have made all 50 dangles.

2. Pass the beading wire through the ring of one half of the clasp and back through the crimp. Make sure that the beading wire is tight around the ring and squeeze the crimp shut. Add a 3mm gold round bead to cover the tail of the beading wire and cut away the excess.

3. Arrange the rest of the loose multistone beads in a line so that the colors are roughly balanced. Add the multistone beads and 44 of the dangles to the wire in a random pattern, making sure that each multistone bead is bracketed by a daisy spacer and each dangle is bracketed by a gold round bead. If you wish to re-create the exact pattern I have used, you can follow this guide, referring to the bead codes in the materials list (D = dangle): ABABA, CDCDC, ABA, CDCDC, ABABABA, CDC, ABABABA, CDC, ABABABA, CDC, ABABA, CDCDCDC, ABABABA, CDCDCDC, ABA, CDC, ABABA, CDC, ABA, CDCDC, ABA, CDCDCDC, ABABA, CDCDCDC, ABA, CDC, ABABABA, CDCDCDC, ABABA, CDCDC, ABABABA, CDCDC, ABA, CDCDCDC, ABABABA, CDCDC, ABA, CDC, ABABA, CDCDCDC, ABABA, CDCDC, ABABA, CDC, ABABABA, CDC.

4. Add a round gold bead and a crimp. Bring the beading wire through the ring of the other side of the clasp and back through the crimp and round bead. Now tighten the necklace so that there are no spaces between the beads, close the crimp, and snip off any remaining beading wire. Add the crimp covers.

TOOLS
Wire Cutters, Crimping Pliers, Round-Nosed Pliers

MATERIALS
- 97 5mm diameter faceted rondel beads (about three quarters of a 16" strand) (B)
- 120 4mm vermeil daisy spacer beads (A)
- 120 3mm seamless hollow gold-filled round beads (C)
- 50 1/2" vermeil headpins with ball tip
- 4 4mm gold-filled jump rings
- 2 gold-filled crimp beads
- 2 gold-filled crimp covers
- 1 vermeil toggle clasp
- 20" of beading wire

5. Add the remaining 6 dangles in the following fashion: Use a jump ring to attach one dangle to the loop of the clasp ring. Use another jump ring to attach a dangle to the previous jump ring. Then use another jump ring to attach a dangle to the previous one. Use the last jump ring to attach 3 dangles to the previous jump ring.

SIMPLY BLUE

LARIMAR, A BLUE VARIETY OF PECTOLITE, IS A NEW GEMSTONE, DISCOVERED ONLY A GENERATION AGO IN THE DOMINICAN REPUBLIC. NAMED BY THE DISCOVERER AFTER HIS DAUGHTER LARISSA AND *MAR*, THE SPANISH WORD FOR "SEA," IT IS FOUND IN NO OTHER PACE ON EARTH AND IS FAMOUSLY REPUTED TO BE THE COLOR OF THE CARIBBEAN SEA. MOST LARIMAR, HOWEVER, EXHIBITS TOO MUCH WHITE, AND IT IS ONE STONE WHERE QUALITY MAKES THE DIFFERENCE BETWEEN SOMETHING GORGEOUS AND SOMETHING A LITTLE BORING. THESE LOVELY BEADS DISPLAY THE UNIQUE WATERY BLUE AND SILKY VITREOUS LUSTER FOR WHICH THE GEM IS JUSTLY ADMIRED.

1. Start the necklace by threading on a crimp. Pass the beading wire through the ring of one half of the clasp and back through the crimp. Make sure that the beading wire is tight around the ring and squeeze the crimp shut.

2. Thread on a 4mm gold round bead, a gold faceted bead, and another 4mm gold round bead so that they cover the tail of the beading wire. Cut away any excess wire.

3. Add a gold rondel bead and a larimar bead. Repeat this pattern 28 times.

4. Add another gold rondel bead, a gold round bead, a gold faceted bead, another gold round bead, and a crimp. Bring the beading wire through the ring on the other side of the clasp and back through the crimp and the three last beads. Now tighten the necklace so that there are no spaces between the beads, close the crimp, and snip off any remaining beading wire. Add the crimp covers.

TOOLS
Crimping Pliers, Wire Cutters, Flat-Nosed Pliers

MATERIALS
29 10mm round larimar beads

30 4mm by 8mm hollow 18 karat gold hand-cast rondels

2 4mm gold-filled seamless hollow round beads

4 2mm gold-filled hollow round beads

2 2mm gold faceted beads

1 18 karat gold hook-and-eye clasp

2 gold-filled crimp beads

2 gold-filled crimp bead covers

20" of beading wire (preferably gold color)

JASPER CHIPS NECKLACE

THE EARTHY CHARACTER OF JASPER IS OFTEN EMPHASIZED BY THE IRREGULARITY OF CHIPS. IN THIS CASE, THE PIECES OF HIDDEN VALLEY JASPER FROM IDAHO LOOK LIKE TINY NATURAL NUGGETS AND ARE PERFECTLY COMPLEMENTED BOTH IN SHAPE AND COLOR BY THE TINY GOLD-PLATED SILVER CHIPS. THE CENTERPIECE STONE IS AN ETCHED AGATE, BUT YOU COULD USE JASPER OR ANY ORGANIC-LOOKING STONE THAT MATCHES THE COLORS OF THE CHIPS.

1. Start by making the centerpiece pendant. Add a vermeil chip to the headpin, then the large agate or jasper centerpiece. Add 5 vermeil chips, using larger ones first. Then add the 2mm round bead. Cut the headpin 3/4" above the last bead and make a wire-wrapped loop.

2. Start the necklace by threading on a crimp. Pass the beading wire through the ring of one half of the clasp and back through the crimp. Make sure that the beading wire is tight around the ring and squeeze the crimp shut.

3. Add a 2.5mm round bead so that it fits over the tail of the wire and cut away any excess. Add a vermeil chip. Then add half of the jasper chips, vermeil chips (reserving 1), and round beads, separating them in a random fashion. At the end of this sequence, use a round bead, a vermeil chip, a round bead, and add the reserved jasper chip.

4. Add a 4mm round bead and then pass the beading wire through the loop of the centerpiece pendant. Check that the length of the necklace is what you want by holding it to your neck. Next add the other 4mm bead and the rest of the jasper and vermeil chips and 2.5mm round beads, starting with a jasper, round, vermeil, round combination and ending with a jasper, vermeil, round.

5. Add a crimp bead. Bring the beading wire through the ring of the other side of the clasp and back through the crimp and the round bead. Tighten the necklace so that there are no spaces between the beads, close the crimp, and snip off any remaining beading wire. Add the crimp covers.

TOOLS
Crimping Pliers, Wire Cutters, Round-Nosed Pliers

MATERIALS

16" of jasper chips approximately 5mm to 10mm wide (half a 32" strand)

1 agate or jasper centerpiece bead approximately 18mm by 13mm

42 3mm to 7mm wide gold-plated (vermeil) Thai chips

28 2.5mm hollow gold-filled round beads

2 4mm seamless hollow gold-filled round beads

1 2mm hollow gold-filled round bead

1 3" vermeil headpin

1 7mm gold-filled ring

2 gold-filled crimp beads

2 gold-filled crimp bead covers

1 vermeil toggle clasp

22" of beading wire

NOTE
Before you begin, it's helpful to divide your vermeil chips and 2.5mm round beads into 2 equal piles and the jasper chips into 2 equal lengths.

CITRINE, GARNET, AND CHAIN NECKLACE

THESE BEAUTIFUL CITRINE DROPS, CUT IN AN UNUSUAL TWISTED
SHAPE, ARE SUCH A STRONG FOCAL POINT OF THE DESIGN THAT
SIMPLE CHAIN SERVES WELL FOR MUCH OF THE LENGTH OF
THE NECKLACE. CHAIN USED IN THIS MANNER ALSO OFFERS A
PLEASANT ECONOMY, REDUCING THE NEED FOR MORE GEMS.

1. Arrange the citrine drops in matching pairs on either side of the largest central bead so that they decline in size as they retreat from the center. Twisted drops are likely to be a little irregular, so do not bother trying to match them exactly; there only needs to be a rough graduation, allowing the central bead to be the focus.

2. Thread a crimp on the beading wire. Pass the wire through the end link of one of the pieces of chain and back through the crimp. Make sure that the beading wire is tight around the link and squeeze the crimp shut. Add a 2mm round gold bead so that it covers the tail of the wire and cut away any excess.

3. Add 5 garnet beads and another gold bead. Starting at the end of the line of citrine beads add 1 of the drops to the wire followed by another gold bead.

4. Add 3 garnet beads, a gold bead, the next citrine drop, and a gold bead. Repeat this pattern 7 more times. Then add the last 5 garnet beads and a gold bead.

5. Add a crimp. Bring the beading wire through the end link of the other piece of chain and back through the crimp and the last 2 gold beads. Tighten the necklace so that there are no spaces between the beads, close the crimp, and snip off any remaining beading wire. Add the crimp covers.

6. Use the jump ring to attach the gold ring to one of the ends of the chain. Open the ring of the lobster clasp and attach it to the other end of the chain.

TOOLS
Wire Cutters, Crimping Pliers, Flat-Nosed Pliers

MATERIALS
9   citrine faceted twisted drops ranging in size from 9mm by 13.5mm to 15mm by 17mm

34   1.5mm faceted round garnet beads

20   2mm hollow gold-filled round beads

2   4½" pieces of cable chain with 5mm links

1   gold-filled lobster clasp

1   6mm gold-filled ring

1   4mm gold-filled jump ring

2   gold-filled crimp beads

2   gold-filled crimp bead covers

7"   of beading wire

TOURMALINE BRIOLETTES NECKLACE

TOURMALINE COMES IN A VARIETY OF COLORS THAT OFTEN BLEND BEAUTIFULLY WITH EACH OTHER. THIS IS A PARTICULARLY LOVELY STRAND OF ALMOND-SHAPED BRIOLETTES THAT CALLS FOR SOMETHING SMALL AND DISCREET THAT STILL MATCHES THE RICHNESS OF THE GEMS; HENCE THE TINY PEARLS AND GOLD BEADS. THIS QUALITY OF TOURMALINE IS NOT INEXPENSIVE, AND THE FLATTENED ALMOND SHAPE HELPS TO PRODUCE A BROAD AREA OF LUSCIOUS GEMSTONE IN THE MOST COST-EFFECTIVE MANNER.

1. Start the necklace by threading on a crimp. Pass the beading wire through the ring of one half of the clasp and back through the crimp. Make sure that the beading wire is tight around the ring and squeeze the crimp shut.

2. Thread on a gold round bead so that it fits over the tail of the wire and cut away any excess. Add 5 pearls, a gold bead, and another pearl.

3. Now add the tourmaline beads in the order you have arranged them, separating each with a pearl, a gold bead, and another pearl.

4. Add a pearl, a gold bead, 5 pearls, and another gold bead. Add a crimp. Bring the beading wire through the ring on the other side of the clasp and back through the crimp and gold bead. Now tighten the necklace so that there are no spaces between the beads, close the crimp, and snip off any remaining beading wire. Add the crimp covers.

TOOLS
Wire Cutters, Crimping Pliers

MATERIALS
39   tourmaline faceted briolettes ranging from 8mm by 11mm to 10mm by 14mm in size

42   3mm 18 karat gold rondel spacer beads

88   2mm pearls

1   18 karat gold toggle clasp

2   gold-filled crimp beads

2   gold-filled crimp bead covers

20"   of beading wire

NOTE
You have probably bought the briolettes on a temporarily strung strand. If the arrangement is how you prefer it, then you can use the beads in the order in which they come off the strand. If you prefer a different lineup, lay out the beads in the order in which you wish to use them. One way to arrange beads of varying size is in graduated order. In this case, however, the color arrangement was far more important to me, and I laid them out in a manner that made a pleasing band of color, allowing the size order to be random.

HYPERSTHENE NECKLACE

RECENT YEARS HAVE SEEN MANY MORE GEMSTONES
PRESSED INTO THE SERVICE OF JEWELRY DESIGNERS, AS
FASHION CONTINUES ITS ENDLESS SEARCH FOR VARIETY.
HYPERSTHENE IS AN ATTRACTIVE DARK GREEN STONE
THAT SOMETIMES EXHIBITS A REDDISH IRIDESCENCE.
A RELATIVELY SOFT AND BRITTLE STONE, HYPERSTHENE
USED TO BE MAINLY THE PROVINCE OF COLLECTORS, BUT
WHEN IT IS CUT INTO SMALL RONDELS IT BECOMES A
DELIGHTFUL ADDITION TO THE JEWELRY DESIGNER'S
PALETTE.

1. Start the necklace by threading on a crimp. Pass the beading
   wire through the ring of one half of the clasp and back through
   the crimp. Make sure that the beading wire is tight around the
   ring and squeeze the crimp shut.

2. Thread on the gold round bead so that it fits over the tail of the
   wire and cut away any excess. Add 7 hypersthene beads.

3. Add a gold tubular bead and 3 hypersthene beads. Repeat this
   pattern 25 more times. Check the length around your neck.

4. Add the last tubular bead and 7 hypersthene beads, the last
   gold round bead, and a crimp. Bring the beading wire through
   the ring of the other side of the clasp and back through the crimp
   and round beads. Tighten the necklace that so there are no
   spaces between the beads, close the crimp, and snip off any
   remaining beading wire. Add the crimp covers.

5. Use the jump ring to attach the charm to the loop of the clasp
   ring.

TOOLS
Wire Cutters, Crimping Pliers,
Flat-Nosed Pliers

MATERIALS (FOR A 15" CHOKER)
92 2mm by 3mm rondel hypersthene beads
27 6.5mm by 4.5mm vermeil tubular beads
 1 11mm diameter vermeil disc charm
 2 3mm hollow gold-filled round beads
 1 5mm gold-filled jump ring
 1 vermeil toggle clasp
 2 gold-filled crimp beads
 2 gold-filled crimp bead covers
19" of beading wire

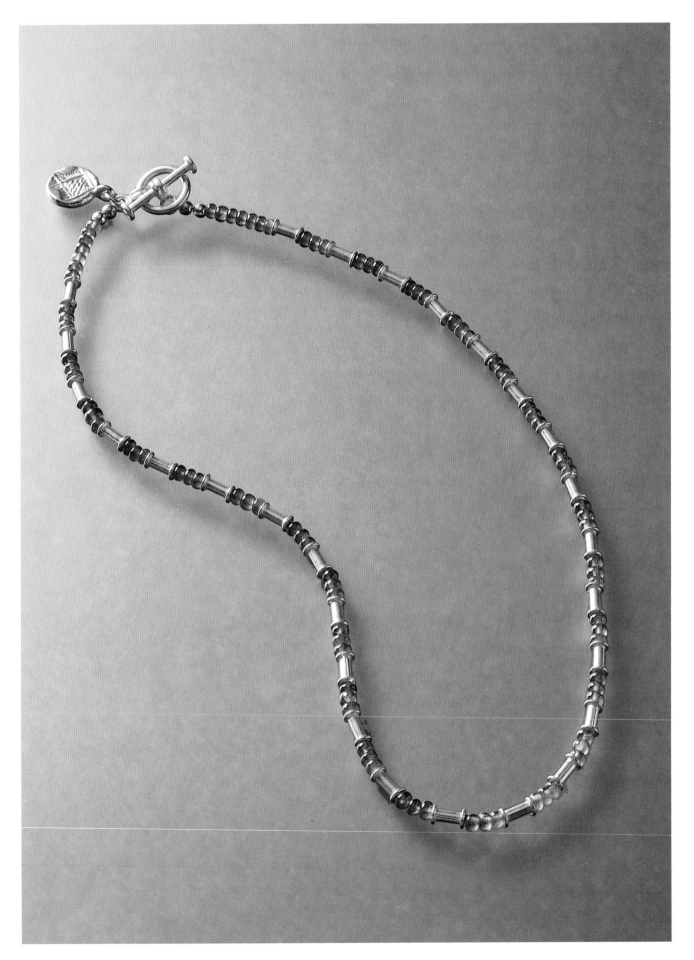

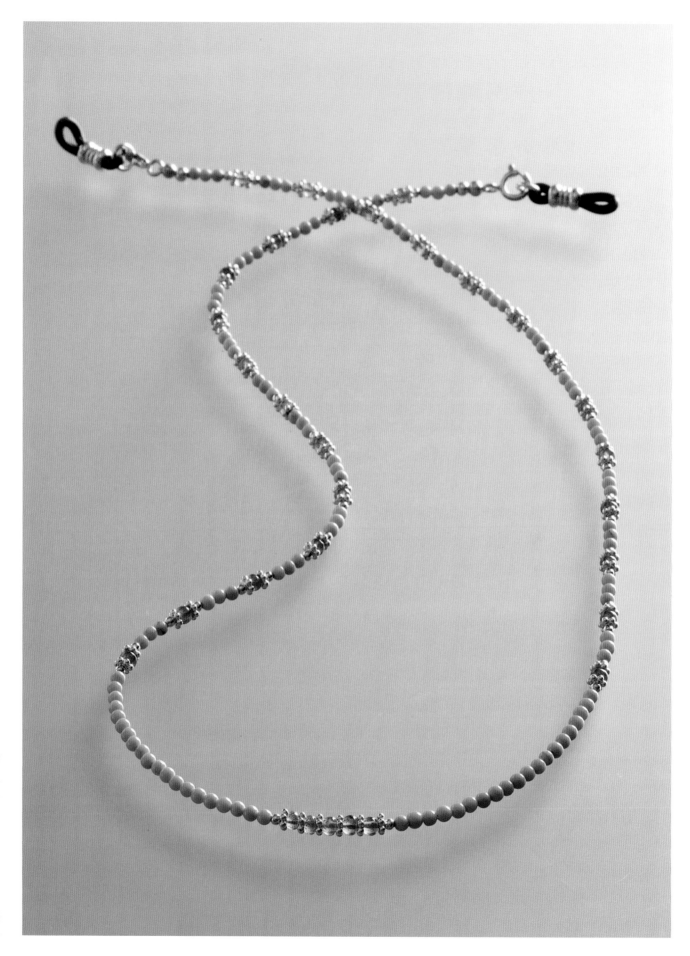

TURQUOISE EYEGLASS LEASH

EYEGLASS LEASHES ARE A WONDERFUL EXCUSE TO WEAR
JEWELRY FOR AN UNQUESTIONABLY PRACTICAL PURPOSE.
I ALWAYS MAKE MINE USING A FINISHING METHOD THAT
ALLOWS THEM TO DOUBLE AS REAL NECKLACES. IN THIS CASE,
I HAVE USED SPRING RING CLASPS AT EITHER END TO CONNECT
THE SPECIAL EYEGLASS HOLDERS. TO USE AS A NECKLACE,
YOU JUST HAVE TO SLIP OFF THE HOLDERS AND ATTACH THE
CLASPS TO EACH OTHER.

1. Start the leash by threading on a crimp. Pass the beading wire
    through the ring of one of the spring ring clasps and back
    through the crimp. Make sure that the beading wire is tight
    around the ring and squeeze the crimp shut. Add the 3mm gold
    bead over both parts of the wire and snip off any remaining tail.

2. Thread on 3 turquoise beads, a 2mm gold bead, a daisy spacer, a
    vesuvianite bead, another daisy spacer, and another 2mm gold
    round bead. Repeat this pattern 12 times and then add 20
    turquoise beads.

3. Add a 2mm gold bead. Then add a daisy spacer and a vesuvianite
    bead and repeat 4 times. Add another daisy and a 2mm gold
    bead, then 20 turquoise beads.

4. Add a 2mm gold bead, a daisy spacer, a vesuvianite bead,
    another daisy spacer, another 2mm gold round bead, and 3
    turquoise beads. Then repeat the pattern 12 times.

5. Add a 3mm gold bead and a crimp. Bring the beading wire
    through the ring of the other spring ring clasp and back through
    the crimp and a round bead. Tighten the necklace so that there
    are no spaces between the beads, close the crimp, and snip off
    any remaining beading wire. Add the crimp covers.

6. Open the jump rings and attach one to each of the eyeglass
    holders. Close the rings and use them to attach the
    eyeglass holders to the spring ring clasps.

TOOLS
Wire Cutters, Crimping Pliers

MATERIALS (FOR A 22" EYEGLASS LEASH)

118	2.5mm Chinese turquoise round beads
31	2mm by 3mm vesuvianite rondel beads
107	2mm hollow gold-filled round beads
60	3mm vermeil daisy spacer beads
2	3mm hollow gold-filled round beads
54	2mm hollow gold-filled round beads
2	gold-filled spring ring clasps
2	gold-filled crimp beads
2	gold-filled crimp bead covers
2	6mm gold-filled jump rings
2	rubber and gold plate eyeglass holders
26"	of beading wire

WHEN GLASS DESERVES GEMS

ALTHOUGH GLASS IS OFTEN USED TO IMITATE GEMSTONES, ARTISTIC SKILL CAN MAKE IT THE EQUAL OF GEMS. HERE, THE GLORIOUS GLASS CENTERPIECE IS IN PERFECT HARMONY WITH THE MOONSTONE GEMS. THIS NECKLACE SHOWCASES A SUPERB EXAMPLE OF THE WORK OF FINE AMERICAN GLASS BEAD ARTIST BRUCE ST. JOHN MAHER. IN THIS LOVELY LANDSCAPE GLASS PENDANT, HE HAS CREATED THE MOON FROM A TINY SLICE OF PRECIOUS OPAL. MOONSTONE WAS THE OBVIOUS COMPLEMENT TO THE PENDANT, BUT BANDS OF PURE WHITE WOULD NOT HAVE WORKED RIGHT BESIDE THE PENDANT, SO I HAVE USED A BRIDGE OF BLACK LEATHER TO CREATE A SUITABLE SPACE BETWEEN THEM. THE TWO DICHROIC BEADS MATCH THE DICHROIC GLASS BRUCE HAS USED AT THE BOTTOM OF HIS PENDANT.

1. Add a leather cord crimp to one end of the leather cord and squeeze it shut. Slip the pendant onto the leather cord, add the other leather crimp to the other end, and squeeze shut.

2. Start the necklace by cutting the beading wire in half and threading a crimp onto the end of one of these wire pieces. Pass the beading wire through the ring of one half of the clasp and back through the crimp. Make sure that the beading wire is tight around the ring and squeeze the crimp shut.

3. Add a 4mm silver round bead so that it fits over the tail of the wire and cut away any excess. Add 4mm black onyx bead and a silver daisy. Add half the moonstone beads, a silver daisy, a 6mm black onyx, a silver daisy, and a dichroic bead. Add a crimp bead. Bring the beading wire through the ring of one of the leather crimps. Tighten the necklace so that there are no spaces between the beads, close the crimp, and snip off any remaining beading wire.

4. Make the other half of the necklace using the directions in steps 2 and 3, attaching the wire to the other half of the clasp and to the other end of the leather. Add the crimp covers.

TOOLS
Wire Cutters, Crimping Pliers, Flat-Nosed Pliers

MATERIALS

1	18mm by 48mm glass pendant bead (Bruce St. John Maher)
10"	of hand-cut 5mm moonstone rondel beads
2	10mm dichroic glass beads
2	4mm black onyx rondel beads
2	6mm black onyx rondel beads
6	5mm silver daisy spacer beads
2	4mm seamless hollow silver round beads
2	silver leather crimps
4	silver crimp beads
4	silver crimp bead covers
4"	of 2mm European-quality black leather
1	silver hook-and-eye clasp
16"	of beading wire

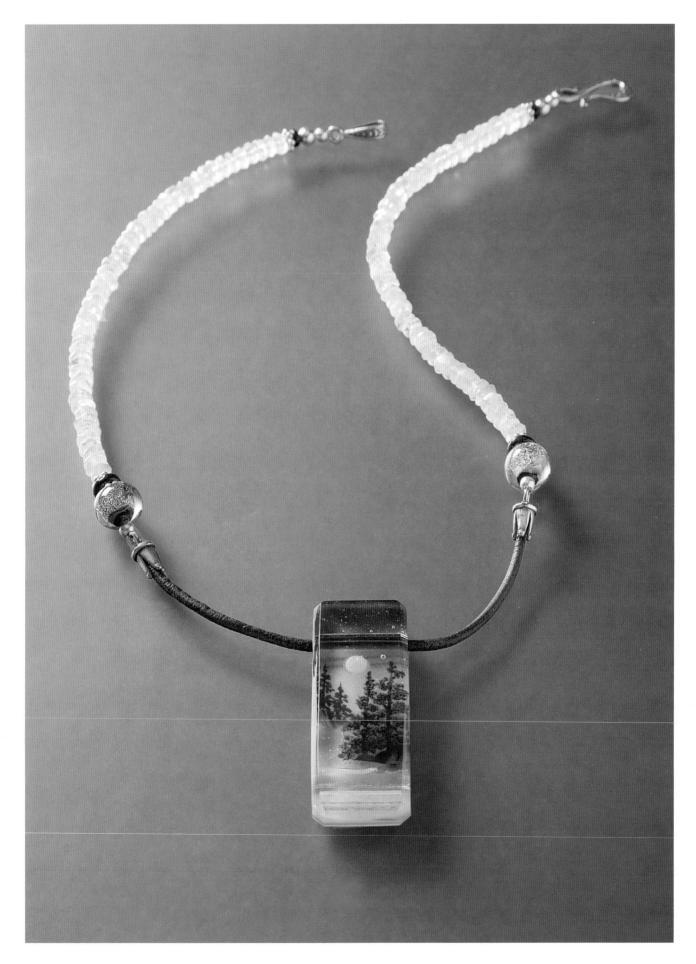

NEW STONES ARE WELCOMED INTO THE   EALM OF GEMS EVERY
                                     ,” A NAME THAT OWES
                                     NTIFIC ACCURACY. IN
                                     WISH IN COLOR, BUT
                                     NENTLY DYED TO
                                     TTRACTIVE BLUE.
                                     OR VERY EXPENSIVE, IT
                                     BEADS LIKE THESE—
                                     OVATION IS HELPING
                                     GHT DESIGNERS AND

imp. Pass the beading
 clasp and back through
 wire is tight around the

t covers the tail of the
e.

n African opal bead, and
pattern 10 times.

bead, and a crimp. Bring
of the other side of the clasp
and back through the crimp and the round bead. Tighten the
necklace so that there are no spaces between the beads, close
the crimp, and snip off any remaining beading wire. Add the
crimp covers.

TOOLS
Crimping Pliers, Wire Cutters

MATERIALS
11	19mm round African opal beads
12	17mm by 3mm silver disc beads
24	2.5mm silver hollow round beads
1	silver toggle clasp
2	silver crimp beads
2	silver crimp bead covers
20"	of beading wire

SLICES OF TOPAZ NECKLACE

CHIPS ARE SOMETIMES AVAILABLE IN UNUSUAL SHAPES, SUCH
AS THESE LOVELY BLUE TOPAZ SLICES. BECAUSE THE EDGES OF
THE SLICES HAVE A GREATER INTENSITY OF COLOR THAN THE
FACES, THIS NECKLACE DESIGN IS A GOOD WAY TO CREATE A
LARGE BAND OF RICH BLUE TOPAZ COLOR AT REASONABLE PRICE.

1. First divide the topaz, peridot, and faceted silver materials into
   even halves. Thread a crimp on the beading wire. Pass the wire
   through the ring of one half of the clasp and back through the
   crimp. Make sure that the beading wire is tight around the ring
   and squeeze the crimp shut. Thread on a 2.5mm silver bead so
   that it fits over the tail of the wire and cut off any excess.

2. Add a peridot bead, 3 faceted silver beads, and a peridot bead.
   Now add half the topaz slices, separating each one by either a
   faceted silver bead or a peridot bead. Space the peridot beads
   evenly on the strand, but not at regular intervals. Save
   1 peridot bead as the last bead of this half of the necklace.

3. When you have used half of all the topaz and peridot beads, add
   the silver ball and make the other half of the necklace in the
   same fashion as the first, starting off with a peridot bead beside
   the silver ball. Save 2 peridot beads for the end. When you have
   used all the topaz slices, check the necklace around your neck to
   make sure both sides are even. Adjust if necessary, then add a
   peridot bead, 3 faceted silver beads, and the final peridot.

4. Add a 2.5mm silver round and the crimp. Bring the beading wire
   through the ring of the other side of the clasp and back through
   the crimp and round bead. Tighten the necklace so that there are
   no spaces between the beads, close the crimp, and snip off any
   remaining beading wire. Add the crimp covers.

TOOLS
Wire Cutters, Crimping Pliers

MATERIALS (FOR A 21" NECKLACE)

1	16" strand of topaz chips averaging about 10mm in diameter
30	2mm peridot faceted round beads
4"	(approximately) of 1mm faceted Thai silver beads
1	20mm Thai silver "woven ball" bead
2	2.5mm hollow silver round beads
1	silver toggle clasp
2	silver crimp beads
2	silver crimp bead covers
25"	of beading wire

GEMS ON A CHAIN BRACELET

THIS DESIGN IS AN EXCELLENT WAY OF USING THE LEFTOVER BEADS FROM PREVIOUS PROJECTS OR TO DISPLAY INDIVIDUAL BEADS THAT YOU FOUND IRRESISTIBLE DURING YOUR LATEST BEAD SHOPPING EXPEDITION. THE MATERIALS LIST SHOWS THE GEMSTONES I HAVE USED, BUT AS IN A CHARM BRACELET, YOU WILL WANT TO USE YOUR OWN SELECTION OF BEADS.

1. Begin by making the dangles. Slip a gemstone bead onto a headpin and choose something of suitable size and design to go with it from your assortment of silver beads. The greater the assortment of silver beads you have nearby, the greater your choice. If the hole of the gemstone bead is bigger than the ball of the headpin, start with a silver bead. Once the little dangle pleases you, cut the headpin about 1/2" above the last bead and make a wire-wrapped loop.

2. Use the jump rings to attach the dangles and the clasp to the links of the chain. Start at the first link and add 2 dangles. Go to the 4th link and add the spring ring part of the clasp. Note: This will form a "tail" on the bracelet that hangs below the clasped part. This is not just a decorative part of the design, but also a practical one. The weight of this tail helps keep the clasped part of the bracelet hanging underneath your wrist so that you don't have to constantly worry that the bracelet is presenting itself properly.

3. Add a dangle on every second link, making sure as you go that they are all on the same side of the chain. Hold up the chain and stretch it out to see that they are hanging consistently. When you have used all your dangles or the bracelet is long enough, cut off any excess links and add the other half of the clasp to the last link.

TOOLS
Round-Nosed Pliers, Flat-Nosed Pliers, Wire Cutters

MATERIALS

7" of 7mm by 5mm silver flat cable chain

19 assorted gemstone beads (Pictured are 3 keishi pearls, 3 blue agate, 2 kyanite coins, 2 tourmaline rectangles, 1 carved lapis lazuli, 2 chrysoprase, 1 blue topaz oval, 1 peridot and amethyst, 1 turquoise set in silver flower, 2 amethyst drops, 1 apatite with opal)

29 assorted silver beads (Pictured are seventeen 2mm hollow round beads, three 4mm hollow round beads, 5 Thai silver chips, 3 bead caps, 1 silver dangle, four 4mm daisy spacer beads)

21 5mm silver jump rings

19 1¼" silver headpins with ball tips

1 8mm silver spring ring clasp

PINK TOURMALINE AND PERIDOT NECKLACE

(Page 122, left)

GEMSTONES OFTEN COME IN GRADUATED STRANDS. BECAUSE IT IS DIFFICULT TO CUT STONES IN PRECISELY THE SAME SIZE, IT IS A USEFUL WAY FOR THE CUTTERS TO TURN INCONSISTENCY INTO AN ADVANTAGE. FOR THE BUYER, THESE STRANDS HAVE TWO ATTRACTIVE QUALITIES: THEY GIVE DESIGNS A HEIGHTENED PERSPECTIVE AND, WHERE EXPENSIVE STONES ARE INVOLVED, PROVIDE SOME ECONOMY. PINK TOURMALINE IS A PARTICULARLY BEAUTIFUL GEMSTONE, AND ITS PRICE CAN INCREASE CONSIDERABLY IN THE LARGER SIZES, SO IT MAKES A LOT OF SENSE TO USE SMALLER BEADS TOWARD THE BACK OF A NECKLACE WHERE THEY ARE LESS NOTICED. THIS PINK AND GREEN AND GOLD COMBINATION CREATES A BRIGHT, LIVELY LOOK THAT IS IDEAL FOR SUMMER OR TROPICAL FASHIONS.

1. Put tape or a bead stopper on one end of the beading wire, and starting at one end of the strand of graduated tourmaline beads, add them to the beading wire until you have strung 7". It is important to keep adding the beads from the strand in a consistent, consecutive manner so that they are gradually increasing in size.

2. Add a gold round bead, a daisy, a peridot bead, and another daisy, then 3 more tourmaline beads. Follow this with another round, daisy, peridot, daisy, round combination.

3. At this point you should be using the beads at the center of your original strand. Make sure that you have 2 of the largest of the tourmaline beads and add tourmaline, round, daisy, peridot, daisy, round, and tourmaline. This is the central part of your necklace.

4. Now add a round, daisy, peridot, daisy, round. And then add 3 tourmaline beads equal in size to the 3 on the other side of the central group. Add 1 more round, daisy, peridot, daisy, round combination.

TOOLS
Wire Cutters, Crimping Pliers, Transparent Adhesive Tape or Bead Stopper

MATERIALS

1	16" graduated strand of 3mm to 4mm pink tourmaline faceted rondel beads
5	6mm round faceted peridot beads
12	2mm hollow gold-filled round beads
10	4mm vermeil daisy spacer beads
1	vermeil lobster clasp
1	7mm gold-filled ring
2	2mm by 2mm gold-filled crimp beads
2	1mm by 1mm gold-filled crimp beads
2	gold-filled crimp bead covers
22"	of size 0.13 beading wire (the tourmaline bead holes are very small)

PAGE 122: Pink Tourmaline and Peridot Necklace (left) and Twice-Around Tourmaline Necklace (right)

5. Continue adding the rest of the tourmaline beads so that they are gradually decreasing in size. When you have used all the beads, lay the necklace out and make sure that the halves are the same length. If they are not even, you can remove beads from one end and add them to the other. Check the length around your neck and add a round gold bead.

6. Now you are ready to add the crimps. When you are using very thin wire, a regular size crimp might not grip tightly enough. To make sure everything is tightly secured, add a small, 1mm x 1mm crimp bead and then slip a larger crimp bead over it (the hole in the large crimp is the same size as the outside of the small crimp). Pass the beading wire through the ring of the clasp and back through the hole of the small crimp and the round bead. Close the crimp and snip off any remaining beading wire. Take the clip or bead stopper off the other end of the necklace and add a round gold bead. Then use the same crimping method to attach the gold-filled ring, making sure before you close the crimp that all the beads sit snugly against each other. Add the crimp covers.

NOTE

The tiny tourmaline beads have very small holes, and it is quite likely that you will have a problem fitting a few of the beads on the beading wire. As you add the beads on the second half of this necklace, the symmetry can be undermined if many of the beads refuse to fit on the wire. Because you don't want to have to take all the beads off the strand, it is best not to start with a clasp. Instead, temporarily clamp one end of the beading wire with a piece of tape or a bead stopper. This way, if you end up with a smaller or greater number of beads on the second half of the necklace, you can easily adjust the first half.

TWICE-AROUND TOURMALINE NECKLACE

(Opposite, right)

TOURMALINE IS ONE OF MY FAVORITE GEMSTONES. ITS VARIOUS COLORS ARE OFTEN BLENDED TOGETHER IN SOFT AND ELEGANT HUES, MAKING IT EASY TO CONVERT AN APPEALING STRAND INTO A SOPHISTICATED NECKLACE. BECAUSE THE COLORS OF THE TOURMALINE SHOULD NOT BE OVERSHADOWED, THE PLAIN WHITE OF PEARLS AND THE YELLOW OF GOLD ARE IDEAL SPACERS. HERE I HAVE USED ONE GOOD-QUALITY STRAND OF TOURMALINE AND AN EQUALLY GOOD-QUALITY STRAND OF SEED PEARLS. BECAUSE THE GEMS ARE ALL VERY SMALL, I HAVE MADE THEM INTO A NECKLACE THAT WRAPS TWICE AROUND THE NECK, PROVIDING A BROADER BAND OF GLITTER.

1. Start the necklace by threading on a crimp. Pass the beading wire through the ring of one half of the toggle end of the clasp and back through the crimp. Make sure that the beading wire is tight around the ring, and squeeze the crimp shut.

2. Thread on a 2mm gold round bead, three pearls, and a 5mm tourmaline heart.

3. Repeat this pattern 104 times, or as many times as you can until the tourmaline hearts are used up. As you go, make sure that the color arrangement of the tourmaline is pleasing. If you liked the arrangement of colors in the strand you started with, keep the same order when completing the necklace.

4. Add a final combination of round gold bead, three pearls, round gold bead, and then the other crimp. Bring the beading wire through the ring of the other side of the clasp and back through the crimp and round bead. Now tighten the necklace so there are no spaces between the beads, close the crimp, and snip off any remaining beading wire.

5. Use the jump ring to attach the wire-wrapped tourmaline heart-shaped pendant to the clasp ring.

TOOLS
Wire Cutters, Crimping Pliers

MATERIALS (FOR A 36" NECKLACE)
1 16" strand of 5mm by 5mm faceted tourmaline heart-shaped beads (about 105 beads)

1 16" strand of 1mm by 2mm white seed pearls

107 2mm hollow gold-filled round beads

1 9mm by 9mm wire-wrapped tourmaline heart-shaped pendant

1 4mm gold-filled jump ring

1 vermeil toggle clasp

2 1mm by 1mm gold-filled crimp beads

40" of size 0.13 beading wire (the tourmaline and pearl holes are very small)

jewelry techniques

BASIC JEWELRY MAKING

During my many years as a jewelry maker, I've found that the following methods work well for me. More importantly, I have found that they work well for the people I have taught and for the thousands of people who have been taught by our Beadworks instructors.

Some of these techniques are simple and require hardly any practice, although dexterity is a big help. Others need patience and several attempts to get them right. If you find yourself becoming frustrated, remember that it is mostly a matter of familiarity. If at first you don't succeed, cut the beads off the thread or wire and start all over again!

There are also many bead stores and educational organizations that offer beading classes. If you are the sort of person who learns best through hands-on teaching, they provide a quick way to get started.

To begin working with beads, you need a well-lit, flat, hard surface with some kind of soft covering to stop the beads from rolling around. If you are going to work at a table or desk, you can buy bead mats or bead design boards or simply use a towel. Personally, I prefer to work on my studio floor, which is well carpeted and allows me to surround myself with tools and beads and a cat to keep me company. Have a mirror nearby so that you can check the look and length of your necklaces and earrings.

Good tools make everything a lot easier. I always use two pairs of flat-nosed pliers, one of them with very narrow jaws. Your round-nosed pliers should have tips narrow enough to make really small loops. If you discover a love for making jewelry, treat yourself to a really good-quality pair of wire cutters.

Once you are seriously into making jewelry, lots of little containers are essential for storing your beads and findings. These can be anything from old jars to specialized bead vials, but it does help if they are transparent and have lids. Multicompartment plastic boxes are also a great storage method.

But don't worry about accumulating lots of tools and gadgets at the beginning. Pick one of the easier designs and just get started!

THE GOLDEN RULES

• The carpenter's maxim is "measure twice, cut once." The wise jewelry maker measures a necklace and bracelet at least twice, and then tries it around the neck or wrist for size. She lays it down and double-checks the pattern. Only then does she make the final knot or squeeze the last crimp bead shut. Never finish off your jewelry until you are absolutely sure it is right!

• Don't let a little clumsy work spoil the whole piece. If you forgive a bad knot or a missed spacer, you will see the flaw every time you wear the jewelry. Better to start over and get it right.

• Don't ruin good ingredients by mixing in poor ones. Even if the material is hidden by the beads or under your hair at the back of your neck, use good quality. (Never, ever, string anything on fishing line!)

• Assume you are going to make mistakes. I constantly make mistakes, even after many, many years of jewelry making! If the instructions call for two headpins, understand that you will need at least two more on standby in case you cut them too short or bend them too badly. If it requires twenty inches of beading wire, make sure you have the rest of the spool nearby in case you need to start all over again.

• Don't waste time looking for the exact bead called for in a set of instructions. Use a substitute of the same quality with similar design values (color, size, shape, texture).

• Never pass up a good bead. If you see one you really, really love, buy it and let it inspire a future design.

USING CRIMP BEADS TO ATTACH CLASPS

Crimps are little hollow tubes that can be crushed together to grip strands of beading wire. You use them like this:

1. Pass the beading wire through the crimp, then through the loop of the clasp and back through the crimp again. With a pair of crimping pliers or flat-nosed pliers, squeeze the crimp until it firmly grips both strands of the wire (Illus. A and B).

2. Snip off the tail of the wire as close to the crimp as possible (Illus. C).

A slightly more sophisticated finish can be achieved by using crimp covers. These fit over the flattened crimp and are gently squeezed shut to create the look of a normal bead. However, you can only use crimp covers if you have previously used crimping pliers to flatten the crimp.

Another trick is to hide the tail of the beading wire inside an adjacent bead(s). I always do this if the hole in those beads is big enough to hold two thicknesses of beading wire, and I often add a spacer bead to the end of my design just to permit this method to be used.

1. Pass the beading wire through one or more beads, then through the crimp and through the loop of the clasp.

2. As you bring the beading wire back through the crimp, push it farther back through the bead(s).

3. Squeeze the crimp shut, and snip the tail of the wire as close as possible to the last bead it was passed through. This way, the tail end of the beading wire will recoil very slightly and be hidden inside the last bead.

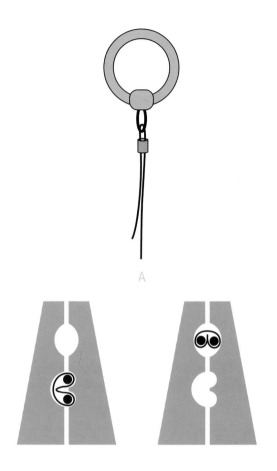

A

B

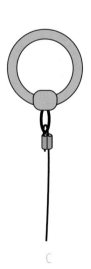

C

USING JUMP RINGS
AND SPLIT RINGS

HOW TO USE JUMP RINGS

1. With a pair of flat-nosed pliers, grip the jump ring so that it lies flat between the pliers with the join slightly to one side of them.

2. Grip the other side of the join with your fingers. Twist the ring sideways so that it opens.

3. After looping the ring through the piece or pieces you are connecting, close it by once again gripping it with the pliers and twisting the wire back until the two ends meet and the join is closed. Make sure that the two ends of the wire are flush with each other.

Never open jump rings by pulling the ends apart, as they will be much more difficult to close. Always twist them sideways as described above.

HOW TO USE SPLIT RINGS

1. Although you can buy a specialty tool to open these, the simplest way is just to slip your fingernail between the split parts of the ring just behind the opening. This should create just enough space to let you push the piece you wish to connect into the split of the ring.

2. Rotate the ring until the connected item has traveled all the way along the split and out of the opposite side. You may want to use your flat-nosed pliers to help rotate the ring.

GETTING KNOTTED: THE ART OF USING SILK THREAD

Strands of beads are sometimes strung on silk thread, which is thought to offer the best compromise between strength and flexibility. It is best to thread the beads onto a doubled strand of silk, both to add strength and to increase the size of the knots. While you can use silk thread without knotting between each bead, it is traditional to make these knots in order to highlight each bead and to prevent them from chafing against each other.

STRINGING ON SILK THREAD

You need a needle to draw the thread through the beads. While any thin needle will do, flexible twisted wire needles make the job a lot easier.

1. Thread the silk through the eye of the needle and draw it through until the doubled length is enough for the necklace (Illus. A). If you are knotting between each bead, your doubled strand should be at least twice as long as the finished necklace. For example, an 18" knotted necklace will require 2 yards, or 72", of silk thread. If you are not knotting between each bead, the doubled thread should be about 6" longer than the finished piece. An 18" necklace will therefore require 4 feet, or 48", of thread.

2. Tie the doubled end of the thread with a simple overhand knot (Illus. B). Pull on the tail with your pliers to tighten the knot.

3. To tighten the knot even more, separate the two threads and pull apart (Illus. C).

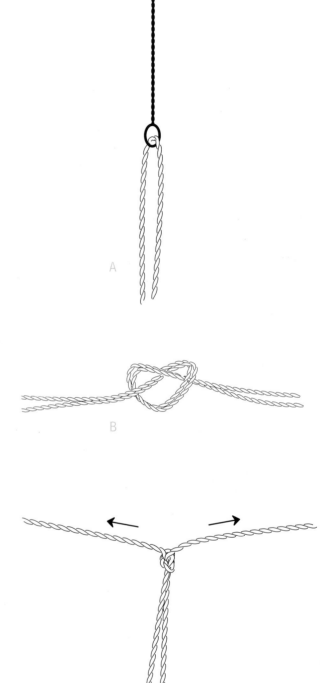

USING AN AWL TO MAKE KNOTS

An awl is a metal needle with a long handle that is used for getting knots to sit snugly against beads or bead tips. It is very simple to use once you know how. You can use the steps below to practice knotting. Once you begin to make a real necklace, you will first have to attach the clasp (page 130).

1. Add a bead to the thread. Make an overhand knot anywhere along the thread, but do not tighten it. Put the point of the awl through the knot, and gently reduce the size of the knot until it fits loosely around the awl (Illus. A). Put your finger on the thread so that the knot lies between your finger and the awl.

2. Keeping your finger on the knot, move the awl toward the bead. You should be able to easily move the knot all the way down the thread until it lies snugly against the bead (Illus. A).

3. Once you have the knot in position, slowly remove the awl as you pull on the thread to tighten the knot (Illus. B).

4. To tighten the knot even more, you can separate the two threads and pull them apart to help force the knot closer to the bead (Illus. C).

5. Add another bead and push it firmly against the knot you have just made. Make another knot as described in steps 1–3. Make sure the beads lie snugly against one another. Continue practicing with a few beads until you are confident that you have the technique mastered.

TOOL TIPS

When you need to knot and can't find your awl, fold out a safety pin and use that.

If you've lost your scissors or can't find your cutters, get out your nail clippers. They are usually very sharp and you can get them nice and close to your bead to cut off excess thread or wire.

A

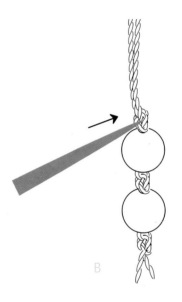

B

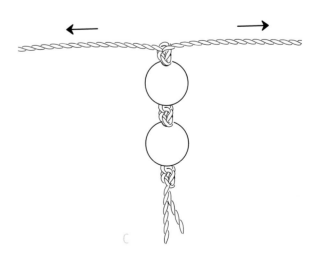

C

USING BEAD TIPS
TO ATTACH CLASPS

When stringing on silk thread (see "Getting Knotted" on page 128), you need to finish off the ends in a way that will let you attach them to the two halves of a clasp. The little findings that enable you to do this are called bead tips. One end of a bead tip is a simple loop that will connect to the clasp. The other end grips the knot at the end of your thread.

To use either kind of bead tip, start with your thread doubled and knotted at the end.

TO USE STRING-THROUGH CLAMSHELL BEAD TIPS

1. Make another overhand knot on top of the first knot at the end of your doubled thread. This is easier to do if you use your awl to guide the loop of the second knot so it sits on the first. Tighten that knot as well. Unless you are very sure of your knots, add a dab of hypo-cement (a clear glue with a precision applicator) or clear nail polish. Trim off the excess tail of the thread with a pair of sharp scissors (Illus. A, B, C, D).

2. Pass your needle and thread into the open clamshell of the bead tip and through the hole at the base of the shell. Pull the thread completely through so that the knot sits snugly inside the clamshell. Using flat-nosed pliers, gently squeeze the sides of the shell together so that it closes around the knot and grips it firmly (Illus. E, F).

3. Make another single knot tight against the bottom of the bead tip. Now add the beads to the length of the silk thread to create your necklace.

4. Once you have finished stringing all the beads of your necklace, finish it off by passing the needle and thread through the hole on the outside of another bead tip. (Remember to make a knot after the last bead.)

5. Pull the thread so that the last knot of your necklace sits firmly against the outside of the bead tip. Now tie an overhand knot so that it sits inside the clamshell of the bead tip. To position the knot properly, use your awl to move the loop of the knot as close to the inside wall of the bead tip as possible. Tighten the knot, pulling the awl out at the last moment.

6. Make a second overhand knot, and tighten it on top of the first. Add a dab of hypo-cement if needed. Using flat-nosed pliers, gently squeeze the sides of the shell together so that it closes around the knot and grips it firmly. Using a sharp pair of scissors, trim off the rest of the thread as close to the outside of the bead tip as possible.

7. You now have a strand with a bead tip at either end. Put the open loop of one bead tip through the ring on one half of the clasp. Use flat-nosed pliers to close the loop so that it is firmly attached to the ring. Attach the other bead tip to the other part of the clasp in the same manner.

TIP

If you add a few smaller beads to the beginning and end of your necklace, it will be easier to undo and close the clasp when you wear it.

QUICK TRICK

If you have an idea for a necklace but don't have the time to make it up, string a few beads defining at least part of the design on a piece of thread or even fishing line and tie off both ends. This way, you will be able to remember what the idea was when you find time to make it.

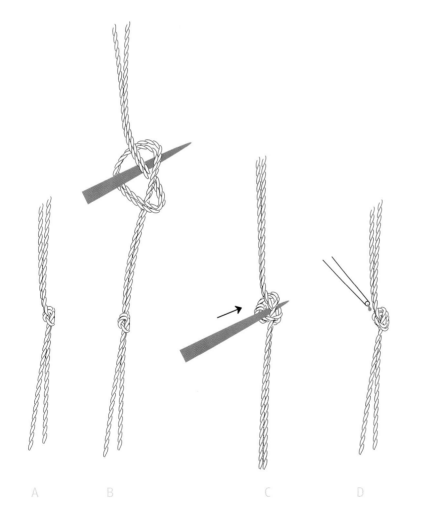

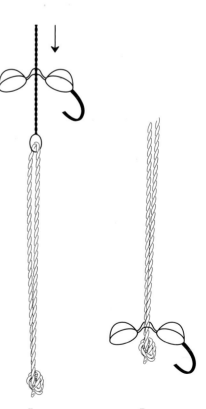

A   B   C   D   E   F

USING BASKET BEAD TIPS

While it is a little more difficult to make the final knot using this style of bead tip, basket beads give a more sophisticated look to your jewelry—if you can master the technique.

1. Take the end of the doubled thread and tie a simple overhand knot. Tighten it by gripping the tail with pliers and pulling. Trim off the excess tail of the thread with a pair of sharp scissors (Illus. A).

2. Pass your needle and thread into the basket and through the hole at its bottom. Pull the thread completely through so that the knot sits snugly inside the bottom of the basket. Put a tiny dab of hypo-cement or clear nail polish on the knot (Illus. B, C, D).

3. Make another overhand knot near the outside of the bead tip, and use your awl to move the loop of that knot tight against the bottom of the basket. This knot keeps the beads from chafing against the bead tip and improves the overall appearance.

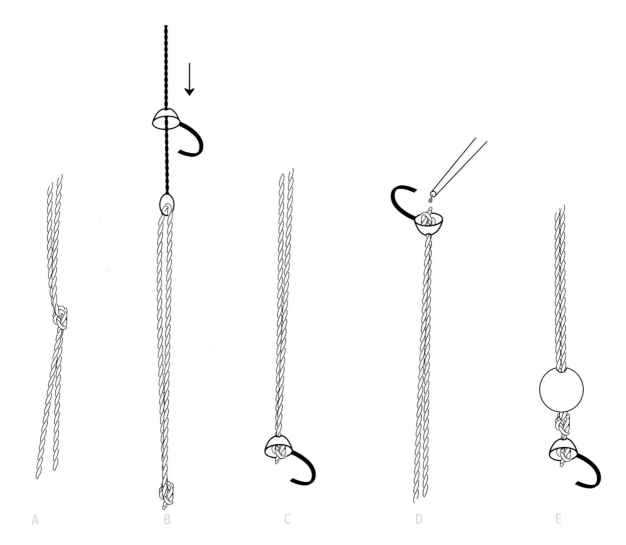

A   B   C   D   E

4.   Now add the beads to the silk thread to create your necklace (Illus. E).

5.   Once you have completed stringing all the beads of your necklace, make an overhand knot, and use the awl to position it tightly against the last bead. Pass the needle and thread through the hole on the outside bottom of another basket bead tip. Pull the thread until the bead tip sits firmly against the knot after the last bead (Illus. F).

6.   Tie an overhand knot, and use your awl to move the loop of the knot as close as possible to the bottom inside wall of the bead tip (Illus. G). Tighten the knot, pulling the awl out at the last moment. It takes a little practice to get this final knot to slip into the basket, but it is important to get a good tight fit so that no thread can be seen once the necklace is complete. Add a tiny dab of hypo-cement or clear nail polish to firmly secure this knot (Illus. H).

7.   Finish off by attaching the ends of the bead tips to the clasp as above (Illus. I, J).

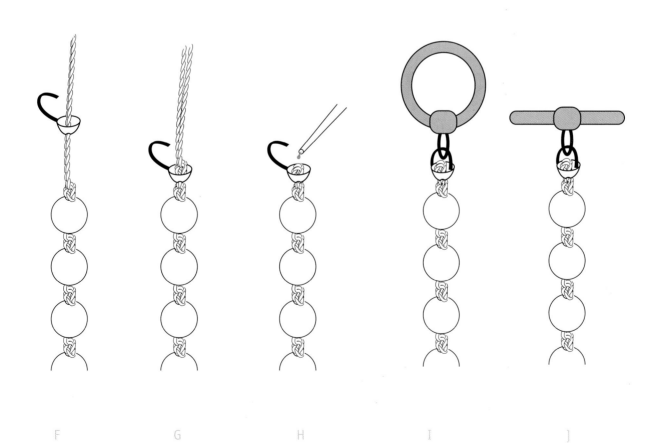

F   G   H   I   J

USING HEADPINS AND EYEPINS

Headpins and eyepins are convenient ways of attaching beads to necklaces, earwires, and other findings. Simply add some beads and make a loop at the top in the following manner:

1. Hold the bottom of the pin to make sure the beads are sitting tightly against it, and cut the top of the pin to the correct length for the loop. For a 3mm loop, there should be a ¼" of pin above the last bead. Small loops are made by gripping the wire toward the tips of the plier jaws. Grip the wire further back to create a larger loop, being sure to allow more wire between the bead and the end of the pin. When you practice this technique, it is useful to make a mark on the jaws of your round-nosed pliers so that you know where to place the wire between the jaws (Illus. A).

2. Grip the top of the pin between the jaws of your round-nosed pliers. Make a "P" shape by rolling the pliers away from you. Move the pliers around if necessary until the tip of the pin meets the wire at the top of the bead (Illus. B).

3. Put your fingernail behind the neck of the "P," where it touches the bead, and bend the loop back until it is centered above the bead. Your finished loop should look like a balloon with the string hanging straight down (Illus. C).

4. To attach the loop to another loop or ring, open it to the side as with a jump ring below (page 127).

NOTE

If you are wire-wrapping on a headpin or eyepin, follow the instructions on the following page, substituting the headpin or eyepin for the wire. For larger loops, allow more distance on the wire. Remember, the wire's placement on the jaws of your pliers determines the size of your loop.

1/4"

A

B

C

WIRE-WRAPPING

This technique can be used with precious metal and other wires or with headpins and eyepins. It forms a stronger loop and adds a space between the loop and the bead. You will need to practice this technique many times to master it. Create a small wire-wrapped loop at each end of a bead in the following manner:

1. Cut a piece of wire to the width of your bead plus about $1\frac{1}{2}$" (Illus. A).

2. With round-nosed pliers, grip the wire about $\frac{1}{2}$" from the end. Bend the wire around the pliers until a loop is formed and the tail of the wire is perpendicular to the stem (Illus. B).

3. With your fingernail behind the loop, use the round-nosed pliers to roll it back until it is centered above the stem of the wire (Illus. C).

4. Using your finger or fingernail, wrap the tail of the wire around the stem a couple of turns. Use flat-nosed pliers to finish wrapping the tail tightly. Snip off any excess wire (Illus. D, E).

5. Place a bead on the wire. Grip the wire so that the jaws are about $\frac{3}{8}$" from the bead, and roll the pliers until a loop is formed and the tail of the wire is perpendicular to the stem (Illus. F, B).

6. With your fingernail behind the loop, roll it back until it is centered above the stem of the wire (Illus. C).

7. Using your finger or fingernail, wrap the tail of the wire around the stem a couple of turns, getting it tight between the bead and the loop. Use flat-nosed pliers to finish wrapping the tail tightly. Snip off any excess wire (Illus. D, E).

NOTE
When making a single loop on a headpin or eyepin, cut the wire about $\frac{5}{8}$" above the bead when making a medium-size loop.

A   B

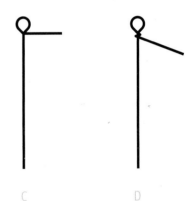

C   D

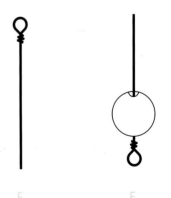

E   F

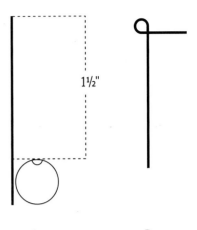1½"

STANDARD MEASUREMENTS

NECKLACE LENGTHS

One of the pleasures of creating your own jewelry is that you can adjust the length of your necklaces so they fit you. A comfortable choker on some necks is a genuine strangler on others, and a centerpiece that is well presented on the faint décolletage of a fashion model might be entirely lost on those who are more generously endowed. If the jewelry is for yourself, disregard the standard lengths and try it on for size as you are making it.

SIZE

The diameter of beads is commonly described in millimeters. Because you often need to work out how many beads to buy for a particular length, it is useful to know how many beads there are per inch, and it is especially useful to know how many beads are in 16", one of the typical lengths of temporarily strung beads. The chart below shows you the number per inch of some common sizes of round beads.

Seed beads, however, are a strange exception to the sensible practice of sizing in millimeters. Keep in mind that there are differences between manufacturers' standards and that the widths of individual seed beads often vary. The chart below also gives a rough guide to their sizes.

APPROXIMATE NUMBER OF BEADS IN:

Bead size		1"	7"	16"	18"
	2mm	12	88	200	225
	3mm	8	59	134	150
	4mm	6	44	100	114
	5mm	5	35	80	90
	6mm	4	29	67	76
	7mm	3.5	25	58	65
	8mm	3	22	50	57
	9mm	2.5	19	45	40
	10mm	2.5	17	40	45
	12mm	2	14	33	38

		Approximate diameter in millimeters	Approximate number of beads in an inch
Seed bead size	15/0	1.4 to 1.5	32 to 35
	13/0	1.6 to 1.7	24 to 27
	11/0	2.0 to 2.1	18 to 19
	8/0	3.0 to 3.1	11 to 12
	6/0	4.0	8 to 9

GETTING THE LENGTH RIGHT

Although you can lay out all your beads in a line and measure them, or place them in the channels of a marked beading board, there is really only one sure way of getting the length right. Just before you think you are halfway through stringing the beads, hold the uncompleted necklace with the clasp at the back of your neck. Looking in a mirror, you can then judge exactly where the strand will fall. This step is critical in any necklace with a centerpiece or a centered pattern, but it is something I do with every single necklace I am making for myself.

THE "STANDARDS"

Although you will decide the right lengths for your own body, it is useful for jewelry makers to have a general reference guide. There are a variety of opinions about terminology and standard lengths. One woman's "long opera" is another's "rope." The following is as good a guide as any, but remember that the best standard lengths are those you create for yourself. Since a bracelet is, to the maker, just a very short necklace, we start with that length.

Bracelet	7 to 8 inches
Choker	13 to 15 inches
Standard short	16 to 17 inches
Standard long	18 to 20 inches
Matinee	About 24 inches
Opera	30 to 40 inches
Rope	40 inches and longer

CLASP LENGTH

A 16-inch strand of beads, knotted with a fish hook clasp will be about 18 inches long when it's finished. If 18 inches isn't long enough, add a few sterling or gold-filled round beads before the clasp. Or if you are using a hook clasp, add some chain to your bead tip on the opposite side to the hook.

BUYING GEMSTONE BEADS

Only twenty years ago, the average consumer would not have had any idea where or how to buy loose gemstone beads. Today there is a vast, sometimes overwhelming, choice of sellers and goods. The Internet alone returns thousands of responses to a search for "gemstone beads"—the majority of the results are sites that want to sell you something. Although websites and mail order catalogs offer a profusion of beads at competitive prices, all is not as simple as it seems, because you cannot consider price without balancing it against quality and the reputation of the seller. Because gemstones are, for the most part, natural material with all the variation that implies, and because most of them have passed through the hands of artisans of varying degrees of skill, each strand is different. Sometimes, as in the case of hematite beads, which are reconstituted and molded in a machine process, the differences are negligible; but with most gemstone beads the variation is, at a minimum, meaningful and, more often, of overriding importance. It may be possible to buy a strand of 4mm faceted sapphire beads for the price of lunch at your local diner, but do not expect them to look anything like a similar-sized strand that sets you back the cost of a suite at the Ritz!

Gem and bead shows give you the opportunity to see a large selection of goods firsthand and to compare quality, but because the sellers leave town in a few days, they are often difficult to track down if the gems turn out to have been wrongly described. So, if you have the opportunity, the first place to turn is to a bead store, one that has both a good range of gemstones and a reputation to uphold.

Whether in stores, shows, or via mail order, gemstone beads are commonly sold as temporarily strung strands. There is no standard length, but 8", 14", and 16" are popular for most shapes, and inexpensive chips are frequently sold in strands of 32" or 36". In making a purchase decision, it is, of course, critical to know the length of the strand, for without it the price can make no sense. Although they may be sold by the strand, the price of more expensive gemstones is calculated by weight, expressed either in grams or in carats, which are one-fifth of a gram. One advantage of shopping in bead stores is that they also have displays of loose beads from which you can buy small quantities. In addition, they should have a range of individual gemstones that can be used as pendants.

WIRE THICKNESS
BEADING WIRES

Because the width of bead holes are expressed in millimeters, you might expect the wires that fit through them to be sized the same way. Unfortunately, most beading wire widths are measured in inches. The following conversion is helpful if you know the size of the bead hole:

0.021 inch = 0.53 millimeters
0.018 inch = 0.45 millimeters
0.015 inch = 0.38 millimeters
0.013 inch = 0.33 millimeters

PRECIOUS METAL WIRES

Although beading wire thicknesses are measured in inches, precious metal wires can be measured in American Standard gauge or inches or millimeters. Confusingly, the higher the gauge number, the thinner the wire. The following conversions help sort it out:

18 gauge = 0.0403 inches = 1.02 millimeters
20 gauge = 0.0320 inches = 0.81 millimeters
22 gauge = 0.0253 inches = 0.64 millimeters
24 gauge = 0.0201 inches = 0.51 millimeters
26 gauge = 0.0159 inches = 0.40 millimeters
28 gauge = 0.0126 inches = 0.32 millimeters

WEIGHT CONVERSIONS
GEMSTONE WEIGHTS

1 carat = 0.2 gram
1 gram = 5 carats = 0.03527 ounces
1 kilogram = 1,000 grams = 2.20 pounds

PRECIOUS METAL WEIGHTS

1 troy ounce = 31.1 grams =
1.10 ounces (avoirdupois)

Wherever you buy your gemstone beads, it is always best to be an educated buyer. The following list gives you an idea of some of the ways that professionals determine value, but because you are unlikely to want to spend much time peering at beads through a magnifying loupe, I first describe a simpler way of discerning quality.

By far the easiest system is just to set two or more strands of differing qualities side by side. In most cases it is immediately obvious which one is more desirable, even though you might not know why—one will just look better than the other. If it doesn't, then you may be quite content with the less expensive strand. The personal worth of a gemstone, unlike its investment value, is entirely dependent on its beauty, and that is in the eye of its owner. Even if the two or three strands that you set beside each other show signs of quality difference, it does not mean that you must necessarily scorn the lower-quality gemstones. Perhaps the differences are not that great, but the prices are. Perhaps even the lowest quality looks good when it is strung around your neck and away from comparison to its superior cousins. These judgments are for you, the wearer, to make, not the gemstone dealer. Where you must rely on the advice of a professional seller, however, is in the matter of enhancements. Because it is almost impossible for the average buyer to detect whether a stone is permanently dyed or heat-treated, whether its surface is smoothed by oil or resin, whether the stone is synthetic or natural, it is vital that the seller give you good advice. There is real value difference between a stone that changes its color after a few months and one that is stable for decades. For this reason, you should only buy gemstones from sellers you trust and who have a good reputation that they wish to protect. Even professional gemstone dealers can be fooled by clever enhancements. You need to know that a caring supplier stands behind the product when you purchase it.

Here are some of the factors professional buyers usually consider when buying gemstones, which might be useful to you in making your own decisions:

• Are the enhancements permanent? Although all emeralds are oiled and many rubies dyed, a quick swipe with a warm, moist, white cloth should reveal little trace of either oil or dye. If the same test on any gemstone reveals traces of dye, you know that the stone will lose some color over time. How much color and how quickly is the question. The seller should be ready to say if any of the enhancements are not permanent (assuming the seller actually knows—most are relying on a chain of trust between them and the gem maker, a chain that is sometimes broken). But keep in mind that, although the poor-quality stone is attempting to look like a better one, it is not masquerading maliciously—the same color in an entirely natural stone will be more expensive. You get what you pay for!

• Are the beads of even size and are all the holes evenly drilled? It is quite easy to tell this with round beads: just stretch the strand out on a soft, flat surface and roll it gently, and any beads that are drilled off-center or that are oddly sized immediately become apparent. With drops and other shapes, hold the strand up to the light and check to see if all the beads hang evenly. Keep in mind that unless the beads are entirely fashioned by machine, there may be some natural variation in size that is either acceptable or appealing.

• How good is the surface quality? Are there any cracks or really serious problems? Blemishes, such as hairline fractures, are common in many stones and some are dipped in oil to gloss over the flaws. Very porous stones, such as turquoise, are sometimes impregnated with resin to harden and protect their surfaces. These are not necessarily deceptive practices, but the buyer needs to know about them.

• Are the inclusions a bonus or a flaw? In diamonds, inclusions reduce value, whereas in rutilated quartz, they increase it. The relationship between inclusions and value in other stones can be complicated and change with time.

• How good is the surface reflection? With some exceptions, the description "lackluster" is as damning to most gemstones as it is to human performance.

• In the case of transparent stones, how good is the clarity and internal reflection? Good clarity greatly increases the value of many gemstones, and the price difference between acceptable and exceptional clarity can be enormous. It is a matter for your personal judgment as to whether the price premium is worth it.

• If the beads are faceted, are the facets regular and even? How much sparkle do they add to the beads? How much has the cutter's skill added to the value of the stone? In general, machine-cut beads are more expensive than hand-cut, but sometimes the latter have a particular charm and might fit better with your design.

• In the case of gems with optical effects, such as iridescence, play-of-color, fire, or chatoyancy (tiger's-eye), how pronounced are these tricks of light? Some stones depend utterly for their value on the quality of these effects—labradorite without much schiller, or labradorescence, is just a gray stone, but when it has plenty, the shimmering blues and greens across its surface make it spectacular.

• And, last but certainly not least, is the color absolutely glorious? Or is it bit too garish or a little too drab? Some gemstone beads have colors so extraordinary that you find yourself lusting after them no matter how the rest of their qualities stack up. Some might be superior in every other way but, if the color doesn't do it for you, you'll probably pass them by.

In judging gemstone beads, you must always keep in mind that none are "perfect" and that, however much they cost, perception of quality is personal. There are times when the cheaper strand might better fit your design plans, as well as your pocketbook.

CARING FOR GEMSTONES

For all their hardness and solidity, gemstones can be vulnerable to the stresses of daily life and need to be properly protected. All gems can break and all, except diamonds, can be scratched. Sometimes the dulling of a stone's surface can be caused by nothing more than the insidious nature of seemingly innocent influences. Although we think of dust as a soft and gentle substance, much of it is composed of tiny quartz particles that have a hardness of 7 on the Mohs scale (Hardness, page 11) and will scratch any softer stone. All gemstone jewelry should be kept in a protective bag, whether it is of soft cloth or simple plastic. Do not throw your gems into a heap in your jewelry box, for one will almost surely scratch another. Rather than trying to remember which gemstones break easily, it is better to realize that they all break and to keep them away from work or sports activities that might cause them harm.

The rays of the sun can cause the colors of some stones, like old soldiers, to simply fade away. While it is easy to understand that enhanced stones are sometimes subject to color deterioration, it is not commonly understood that many natural gemstones are also susceptible. Yet stones like amethyst, chalcedony, coral, and kunzite can all fade in simple daylight. So, unless they are diamonds, don't wear gems during a lengthy sunbathing session and, if you live in a hot, sunny climate, any stones vulnerable to color change should be saved for indoor or evening wear.

Even water can be a threat. Opaque, noncrystalline stones are porous and will happily suck up water and any nasty chemicals dissolved in it. Don't jump in the hot tub or shower with your jewelry on. Don't do the dishes wearing a gemstone bracelet. Don't go swimming in your pearls—they come from the sea, and their little calcium carbonate hearts would love to dissolve back into the ocean. But, while gemstones are better kept out of water, many of them depend on the stuff and suffer if they dry out, so keep your jewelry in a place that has at least a little humidity—it won't hurt any of them and will soothe those like opals and pearls that fear drying out.

Some gems are easily damaged by acids, cosmetics, hair sprays, and so on, so it is safest, for all gemstone jewelry, to use the old adage for pearls, "Put them on last and take them off first." This way they are less likely to receive a gratuitous shower of hair spray or perfume.

CLEANING GEMSTONES

If you use the guidelines above for wearing and storing your gemstones, they should remain in their pristine state for a very long time. Unfortunately the same cannot be said for the silver and low-karat gold that might accompany them. Tarnish needs to be removed, and gemstones can make that a difficult task. A few gems, such as rubies, sapphires, and diamonds, can stand being plunged into liquid silver and gold cleaners, but the great majority cannot. So, do not even think about it! (If your rubies contain any color-enhancing dye, you will certainly find out about it when they are bathed in chemicals, and you will wish you had not.) Ultrasonic cleaners might allow the very hardest gems to survive, but you are taking a chance putting anything less than diamonds, sapphires, and rubies into them—so don't.

A better method for cleaning is to treat the precious metals and the gemstones separately. Use a silver or gold cleaning cloth to remove tarnish from the metallic elements, then clean the gemstones with a very soft toothbrush dipped in a weak solution of water and very mild soap. Pat them dry with an absorbent towel. Think of the metallic bits as teenagers who can only benefit from a good scrubbing and the gemstones as babies whose tender skin demands the gentlest of care.

SOME STONES THAT REQUIRE EXTRA-SPECIAL CARE

Opals: Soft and containing significant amounts of water, opals are among the most delicate of gemstones. Great care should be taken to avoid an environment where they will dry out, for they will crack and lose their beauty. Opals are notorious for falling out of their settings, breaking, and losing their color; storing in moist absorbent cotton is often advised.

Turquoise: The natural color of the stone can be changed by heat, strong light, and cosmetics and detergents. Turquoise is both porous and water-containing, so it can absorb damaging liquids, and drying out can cause cracking. The stone is relatively soft and easily scratched.

Amber and jet: Since it is a fossilized tree resin, amber is extremely soft and can be scratched by a fingernail. It is sensitive to heat and can be burned, like incense, by the flame of a simple match. Acids, alcohol, and many other chemicals can cause damage. Jet is similar to amber in vulnerability.

Coral and pearls: These are both soft and vulnerable to scratching. Composed of calcium carbonate, they will dissolve in acids. Store them carefully and keep them away from chemicals and polluted air.

Lapis lazuli: This stone is sensitive to chemicals, hot water, acid, and alkali. Keep it away when performing household chores.

Chrysacolla, rhodochrosite, malachite, and howlite: Are all soft and easily scratched.

Tourmaline: Has the strange quality of attracting dust and dirt when it is rubbed or heated. Keep it in a protective pouch and wipe it clean more frequently than other gems.

RESOURCES

Many of the materials for these designs, as well as the locations of Beadworks stores, can be found online at www.beadworks.com.

There are several Internet directories of bead stores, including www.guidetobeadwork.com. The website www.mapmuse.com quickly finds a bead store location near you if you go to "crafts" and then to "beading shops."

A number of publications serve the bead customer and have large resource listings:

Bead & Button Magazine: www.beadandbutton.com

Beadwork Magazine: www.interweave.com/bead/beadwork_magazine

Bead Style: www.beadstylemag.com

For information or further education about gemstones, the following sites might be of interest:

The Gemological Institute of America: www.gia.edu

The Gemmological Association of Great Britain: www.gem-a.info

The Gemmological Association of Australia: www.gem.org.au

The Smithsonian, National Gem and Mineral Collection: www.mineralsciences.si.edu/collections.htm

American Gem Trade Association: www.agta.org

Due to the rapid growth of bead stores in the past twenty years, there is now a wide selection of places to buy beads, findings, and threading materials. In North America alone, there are more than a thousand bead stores, as well as dozens of Internet retailers. Although shopping online can be quick and convenient, nothing beats the experience of being in a well-stocked bead store. There you are able to feel the texture of the beads and arrange them side by side to see if the combinations please you. If you cannot find exactly the bead you are looking for, don't be afraid of making suitable substitutions for materials in the designs. By adding some of your own creative judgment, you end up with a piece of jewelry that is uniquely yours.

ACKNOWLEDGMENTS

The jewelry in this book was designed and created by Nancy Alden.

Thanks to the following people for their work on the book:
Jennifer Lévy, photography
Ariana Beaudoin, jewelry model
Abigail Wall, gemstone sourcing
Stephen Sammons, research
Everyone at Potter Craft, including Rosy Ngo, Chi Ling Moy, Melissa Bonventre, Rebecca Behan, and La Tricia Watford.

I would also like to thank the editors and designers of this and previous books in the series for their meticulous and inspired work forming my text and jewelry into such a delightful visual treat for the reader.

This book is dedicated to the miners, cutters, and polishers of gemstones whose hard work provides us fortunate jewelry makers with the elements of our designs. Their labor and skills make possible the art of gemstone jewelry.

ABOUT THE AUTHOR

Nancy Alden is a jewelry designer and cofounder of the Beadworks Group, one of the world's largest retailers of beads. As Beadworks' principal buyer and designer, she has traveled the world in search of the most beautiful components for jewelry design. She is as at home with gemstone merchants in Jaipur, silver makers in Bali, and glass artists in Bohemia as she is with pearl producers in China. Her knowledge of beads and findings is unrivaled, spanning all categories of material and all stages of production, from the creation of a single bead to its final role in a finished piece of jewelry.

Starting as a silver and goldsmith, Nancy turned to designing with beads because of the vastly greater possibilities for creative expression. Having seen the world of jewelry design open for herself, she then went on to introduce other people to the creative pleasures and the economies of making their own jewelry. By creating Beadworks classes and sharing her skills with other instructors, she has generated a network of teachers who have added to the ever-growing number of women and men able to design and create jewelry. When she is not in search of new beads, Nancy divides her time between her home in Connecticut and her studio retreats in Europe and the Grenadines.

If you are inspired by the designs in this book, but too busy to make them yourself, visit www.NancyAlden.com for a range of gemstone jewelry.

ABOUT BEADWORKS

In 1978, a small store in London began selling a very ancient product in a very novel way. Although beads are among the very earliest of traded articles, the concept of offering a large, sophisticated, and open display to the general public was new. The shop never advertised—indeed, it didn't even have a name for many years—but the demand for its products was immediate and overwhelming. Simply by word of mouth, the original store became world famous.

With American jewelry designer Nancy Alden, the concept expanded to North America, where it has grown to half a dozen stores and a mail-order business. Beadworks has inspired people from around the world to open their own bead stores, enabling hundreds of thousands of people to make their own jewelry. You can visit Beadworks online at www.beadworks.com.

INDEX